Durable Plants for the Garden

A Plant Select Guide

Plant Select®
Colorado State University
Denver Botanic Gardens
Green Industries of Colorado

EDITED BY James E. Henrich

FULCRUM
GOLDEN, COLORADO

Cover, front flap: SPANISH PEAKS
foxglove.

Cover, front, from top left: Corsican
violet, SILVER BLADE evening
primrose, TABLE MOUNTAIN ice plant,
Corsican violet, prairie cordgrass,
Turkish veronica, bluestem joint fir,
moon carrot, wild thing sage.

Cover, back flap: PURPLE MOUNTAIN
sun daisy.

Previous page, clockwise from top
left: Sea Foam artemisia, SONORAN
SUNSET hyssop, Snow Angel coral
bells, Ruby Moon hyacinth bean.

Text © 2009 Plant Select®

Plant Select® is a Colorado nonprofit corporation.

Library of Congress Cataloging-in-Publication Data

Durable plants for the garden : a Plant Select guide / edited by James
E. Henrich.
    p. cm.
 Includes bibliographical references and index.
 ISBN 978-1-55591-590-2 (pbk.)
 1. Alpine garden plants--Rocky Mountains. I. Henrich, James E.
 SB421.D87 2009
 635.90978--dc22
                                        2008024140

Printed in Singapore by Imago
0 9 8 7 6 5 4 3 2 1

Design: Ann W. Douden
Plant Select® Editor: James E. Henrich

FULCRUM PUBLISHING
4690 Table Mountain Drive, Suite 100
Golden, Colorado 80403
800-992-2908 • 303-277-1623
www.fulcrumbooks.com

Dedicated to Harry Swift,

avid plantsman and nurseryman who pioneered the way

for commercial production of native plants in Colorado.

In memory of Dr. Melvern F. Tessene (1941–2007),

esteemed botanist and plantsman who dedicated his

life to commercial plant breeding and seed production.

He produced seeds for Plant Select and provided expert

counsel about professional methods of plant introduction.

Agastache rupestris, Sᴜɴꜱᴇᴛ hyssop.

Contents

Salvia pachyphylla, Mojave sage, with two-tailed swallowtail butterflies.

The Roots of Plant Select

Plant Select is a program designed to seek out and distribute the very best plants for gardens from the High Plains to the intermountain region. Plant Select is a cooperative program administered by Denver Botanic Gardens and Colorado State University together with landscape and nursery professionals from throughout the Rocky Mountain region and beyond.

—Plant Select Mission Statement

Plant Select for the Rocky Mountain and Plains States   *by James E. Henrich*

Plant Select is a very successful plant introduction and promotion program in the Rocky Mountain and plains states that started more than twenty-five years ago as a joint effort of the staff at Denver Botanic Gardens (DBG) and Colorado State University (CSU), with assistance from members of the green industry. Initially, the program was envisioned primarily to introduce outstanding woody plants from the region for commercial sale through the local green industry.

The program struggled for many years, but in 1996 a pivotal change occurred that helped to spark the program into action. Its impetus was an insightful recommendation from a keystone member of the green industry: focus primarily on promoting novel perennial plants in addition to woody species. The recommendation also included production of a color brochure. The new focus immediately galvanized cooperation from local green industry members with national distribution potential. Without the green industry's promotional machinery, the program would not be what it is today.

Until late 2006, at which time Plant Select became a Colorado corporation, it was equally admin- istered by the three cooperating entities. Under the new organizational structure, a six-member board of directors comprised of two representatives from each of the three participating agencies oversees its opera- tion, replacing the former advisory committee. Two standing committees, propagation and marketing, have been active throughout the program's history; ad hoc committees (for example, publications, pho- tography, trial gardens, and plant exploration) are created as needed. In 2008 the program's first full- time paid position was created; the executive director is responsible for administering the program.

Plant Selection, Sources, and Evaluation

Criteria for selecting the plants for the program include performance in a broad range of garden situ- ations in the Rocky Mountain region, adaptation to the region's challenging climate, uniqueness of flower color or plant habit, disease and insect resistance, exceptional performance under low water conditions, a long season of beauty in the garden with an empha- sis on fall color, interesting fruit, and winter appeal, noninvasiveness, and capability to be mass produced.

Germplasm for the program from 1997 to 2007 has been selected from the outstanding living collec- tions held at DBG, existing highly desirable landscape plants that simply needed commercial promotion, the commercial sector, and regional USDA plant introduc- tion stations. Original acquisition methods include selections from regional and international field col- lecting ventures by DBG staff, selections of natural sports within populations of commercially available cultivars, and botanical gardens' seed lists. A limited number of promotions have been the result of selec- tions from plant breeding programs.

Any committee member can recommend a plant for inclusion in the program, and a cumulative working list of species is retained for future consid- eration. Sample germplasm is distributed for trial at various locations throughout Colorado, where prospective selections are evaluated for a minimum of three to five years before being released for sale. Each year the preliminary list of potential candidates is evaluated at a meeting during which the sponsor details the rationale for consideration. During the

Plant Research Stations

Over the course of time, USDA plant research and field stations have played critical roles in regional plant evaluation. The focus of their research has typically been evaluation of plant species for use as food or ornamental application, or for shelterbelts, soil erosion control, revegetation, and conservation needs. However these facilities sometimes need assistance distributing their phenomenal plants to alternative beneficiaries.

Two regional plant research stations have been extremely invaluable resources to the Plant Select program: High Plains Arboretum and Upper Colorado Environmental Plant Center. The former is located in southeastern Wyoming near Cheyenne and the latter in northwestern Colorado near Meeker. Both are situated in areas with similar environmental and geographical constraints: high wind, aridity (less than 15 inches of annual precipitation), altitude above 6,000 feet, low humidity, low winter snow cover, and alkaline soils. High Plains Arboretum has the added "blessing" of being located in an area with the highest incidence of hailstorms in the United States.

Plants tested at these sites must generally be able to tolerate the harsh natural conditions and survive with little supplemental care, such as water and fertilizer. It has often been said that if plants can survive at these stations, they can survive anywhere.

Since its founding in 1928, the High Plains Arboretum has evaluated 1,300 kinds of woody ornamental plants, 200 kinds of trees and shrubs for windbreaks, 2,000 fruit varieties, and 8,000 vegetable varieties. Plant Select has acquired germplasm of the following species from this arboretum's living collection: *Buddleja alternifolia* 'Argentea', *Lonicera korolkowii* 'Floribunda', *Philadelphus lewisii*, *Ribes uva-crispa* 'Red Jacket', and *Sibiraea laevigata*. Although Plant Select has not yet selected plants for introduction from among the grass and woody living collections at the Upper Colorado Environmental Plant Center, it is considered an untapped resource.

The pioneering spirit upon which field stations such as those at Cheyenne and Meeker are established is a true testament to the dedication, leadership, and vision of their staffs to evaluate and introduce plants that will enhance people's lives. The living collections of such stations are extremely valuable resources and must be protected for posterity.

growing season, an evaluation of potential and final candidates is conducted by a broad representation of participating members. Sufficient availability of germplasm and speed of production are important additional criteria. To accommodate production failures, more candidates are carried each year than can be promoted.

Naming, Production, and Royalties

Cultivar names are established for selections that warrant such distinction; trademark names linking the promotion with the Plant Select program are filed with the US Patent and Trademark Office, while selections with a unique genotypic character receive a name for which a patent is sought. Names are selected primarily on the basis of their association with the Rocky Mountain region (for example, Red Rocks, Pikes Peak, Mesa Verde, Pawnee Buttes). A secondary consideration is to choose names that have not been previously associated with a plant.

One or more commercial participants takes responsibility for increasing the germplasm stock to predetermined numbers required for distribution and sales. Seed germplasm is generally produced by a single member, while vegetative germplasm is propagated by several members of the production team. Each selection is actively promoted for five years.

Commercial organizations pay membership dues to Plant Select to secure rights to the popular promotional selections. Additionally, royalties are paid to Plant Select for the sale of each plant. Royalty values vary depending on whether the plant is an introduction or recommendation, an annual, perennial, or woody species, or trademarked or patented.

Promotion

Each year the new introductions are widely promoted in four-color brochures, in newspaper articles, on radio talk shows, on banners and posters at garden centers, and at local, state, regional, and national horticultural conferences. Plants are donated to public demonstration gardens throughout the Front Range and beyond. Managers of the demonstration gardens conduct ongoing evaluations of each variety's performance, submitting their reports to the program.

Since the flagship promotion in 1997, seventy-four selections have been featured through 2007 and more than 5 million plants have been sold. Plant Select has succeeded because of the outstanding talents of the participating organizations and members, foremost of which is unconditional, nonproprietary cooperation. DBG and CSU staffs and the active nursery and garden center participants of Plant Select share one unifying goal: passionate promotion and introduction of exceptional plants for the Rocky Mountain region and beyond.

James E. Henrich is a horticultural consultant in Denver, Colorado. He was formerly the assistant director of the Conservatory of Flowers and San Francisco Botanical Garden in San Francisco, California, director of horticulture at Denver Botanic Gardens in Denver, Colorado, and horticultural coordinator at Missouri Botanical Garden in St. Louis, Missouri.

Plant Select and Colorado State University   *by James E. Klett*

Colorado State University (CSU) has been committed to Plant Select since the early 1980s, long before the program went public in 1997. CSU is the land grant university of Colorado with a mission to extend "knowledge to grow by" to the citizens of Colorado and beyond. Plant Select fits perfectly within this purpose to educate about new and better-adapted plants. The Agricultural Experiment Station, an integral part of CSU, initiated a project in the early 1980s titled Introduction and Evaluation of Landscape Plants for Colorado and the Rocky Mountain Region. CSU realized that a joint effort with Denver Botanic Gardens (DBG) and the green industries of Colorado would bring success to their mission of evaluating, recommending, and introducing landscape plants for this region.

Considerable time was spent among the three partners in the 1980s and early 1990s as they worked through all the processes needed to initiate such a program, as well as eventually deciding on the name Plant Select. The ongoing evaluation research on landscape plants at CSU served as an initial resource.

Woody plant and herbaceous perennial evaluation plots were established in the early 1980s at the Plant Environmental Research Center (PERC) on the CSU campus. The center includes a 7-acre arboretum for woody-plant testing and evaluation and more than an acre of herbaceous perennial evaluation trials. Several thousand plant taxa have been evaluated over the years. This critical plant evaluation knowledge is utilized in discussions among Plant Select committee members to identify Plant Select plants.

A memorandum of agreement was signed between CSU and DBG in the mid-1990s to formally initiate this program in cooperation with the green industries of Colorado. Both institutions had responsibilities outlined in the memorandum. CSU took leadership in coordinating the administration of the program by organizing the meetings, taking minutes, and setting agendas.

Over the years, CSU has played a vital role in the evaluation of future Plant Select herbaceous and woody plants. Herbaceous plants have and continue to be evaluated in trial plots at PERC and at the annual flower trial gardens, located on the Fort Collins main campus. Woody-plant trials have been initiated throughout Colorado for the evaluation of potential Plant Select woody plants. Graduate students have been involved in replicated research at five different climatic sites throughout Colorado. These research data are critical to maintain the integrity and credibility of the program. The data gathered from these plots help Plant Select make research-based decisions on future plant recommendations and introductions. Some potential new clones and patentable plants are also forthcoming from these research plots.

As the program grew and prospered, student hourly labor was needed to help the program function smoothly; this assistance has grown in recent years. Students also help record data and maintain plant evaluation plots. Graduate students have also researched sexual and asexual propagation techniques as well as cultural challenges of several Plant Select introductions. This research has led to the development of propagation protocols that help our grower members successfully propagate and produce Plant Select plants.

As Plant Select grew, the need for patenting and trademarking plants designated as program recommendations and introductions became evident. Under the direction of the advisory committee, CSU implemented, and continues to implement, its directives with the appropriate professional authorities. Royalties received from the sale of these plants help ensure an ongoing resource for research, development, and continuation of the Plant Select program.

Marketing of Plant Select has grown yearly, and CSU has been involved actively in many marketing decisions. CSU has taken the leadership role in organizing the annual demonstration garden meeting, where new plants are distributed to demonstration garden participants and information about plant performance is exchanged. This program has grown to be an all-day event, with staff attending from approximately ninety demonstration gardens from around Colorado and neighboring states. Plant growth and adaptability data, along with information on other cultural factors, are collected from all of these sites at the end of each growing season and placed on the Plant Select website. The information gained from the demonstration gardens is helpful to all Plant Select members and is distributed to gardeners throughout Colorado by horticultural agents.

CSU has managed the website from the inception of Plant Select. The extension information technology person has been essential to the development of the site and regularly updates it. CSU administers Plant Select memberships by processing annual dues statements and providing marketing material to the entire grower and retail membership base.

CSU is a vital part of Plant Select. The university is dedicated to help improve the quality of life and economic development for all Coloradans. Plant Select plays an important role in this development by providing new and underused adaptable landscape plants for all its citizens. This program stands as a vital component of CSU's partnership programs, dedicated to setting the standard as a twenty-first-century land grant university by serving the public and addressing the challenges of our time.

James E. Klett is professor and extension landscape horticulturist in the Department of Horticulture and Landscape Architecture at Colorado State University in Fort Collins, Colorado.

Staff at Denver Botanic Gardens (DBG) have not only helped conceive the Plant Select program but have participated enthusiastically in all facets of Plant Select since the beginning. This relatively young urban garden hosts several key meetings of the program every year. A large share of the plants in Plant Select derive from the diverse palette of plants that make up DBG's substantial plant collections. It might even be said that an important impetus in the creation of Plant Select was the need to create an orderly and equitable way of dispersing the veritable flood of novel horticultural plants that were accumulated at DBG during the 1980s and 1990s.

DBG was founded in 1951 when the Colorado Forestry and Horticulture Association incorporated as a nonprofit corporation to oversee a 100-acre botanic garden site within City Park. This site could not be secured by fencing, and in 1959 ground was broken at the present York Street site. DBG is a 23-acre urban garden designed by Garrett Eckbo of EDAW (an architecture, environment, and landscape design company) to display a spectrum of horticultural methodologies and plant collections "From Tropics to Tundra," meaning from equatorial rain forest in the tropical conservatory to alpine plants in the Rock Alpine Garden and on Mt. Goliath (a mountain peak section near the summit of Mt. Evans).

Today, DBG is comprised of several dozen highly sophisticated gardens that exemplify a variety of horticultural styles, from formal gardening at Centennial Park to the naturalistic, revegetated short-grass prairie habitats of Chatfield Arboretum and the Laura Smith Porter Plains Garden at York Street. Nearly 20,000 kinds of plants are skillfully combined in these gardens. Horticulturists attempt to site each of these plants to ensure optimal growth while combining them with other plants to both mimic the ecological associations the plant has in nature and to create artistic combinations that delight visitors throughout the growing season. This is no easy task.

At first, most of the plants and gardens at DBG were derived from what could be purchased from garden centers locally and through mail-order nurseries in the Midwest and on the coasts, which is to say that the basic palette of DBG's first years consisted of plants from maritime climates needing copious and consistent irrigation. As the vision for DBG evolved, the mission to connect people with plants, especially plants from the Rocky Mountain region and similar climatic regions around the world, inspired the notion of seeking out more drought-adapted native plants and exotics from steppe climates in other parts of the world. A severe drought in the late 1970s along with a major capital campaign resulted in the creation of the Rock Alpine Garden in 1980, and a series of native gardens in the ensuing decade set the stage for a transformation. DBG's staff sought out thousands of plants from throughout the West and through seed exchanges and specialist collectors to furnish these novel gardens. By the turn of the millennium, DBG was acknowledged as having the finest collections of native plants of the intermountain, Rocky Mountain, and Great Plains regions; geographically, this amounts to almost half of the continental United States.

A remarkable assemblage of gardens has evolved at DBG that is truly different from those found at the hundreds of botanic gardens elsewhere in the United States and the thousand or so found elsewhere around the world. I know of no public garden that possesses such an extraordinary range of plant collections: thousands of species and hybrids of orchids and bromeliads in an artistic conservatory; dozens of varied gardens from classic Japanese in *Shofu-en* to Chinese-flavored in Plantasia. DBG takes pride in maintaining the most extensive water and alpine gardens in North America, as well as an astonishing range of herbaceous collections, from classic English borders to several acres of unirrigated native plantings that run the gamut from prairie to near-desert succulent collections.

Few public gardens with extensive plant collections approach DBG's sensitivity of artistic design, found in its carefully color-coordinated borders and brash modernistic annual bedding schemes. The

Silver fountain butterfly bush.

very artistry of these gardens is perhaps the ingredient that has propelled so many plants into Plant Select and thereby into home gardens around the world. Few public gardens have forged the powerful partnerships DBG has, with CSU and wholesale nurseries across North America. These partnerships have demonstrated DBG's relevance and credibility among the Rocky Mountain community. Homeowners know that DBG's spectacular displays are dedicated not to abstract research and recondite display but to providing the region with better plants for home gardens.

It is hard to imagine the impact DBG plants have had on the local horticultural scene. In 1980 you would have been hard-pressed to find any penstemon sold in the Front Range area aside from *Penstemon pinifolius* or an occasional Viehmeyer hybrid such as 'Prairie Dawn'. Today there are Front Range garden centers that offer several dozen kinds of penstemons. I doubt that this would have occurred if DBG had not been promoting, displaying, and selling nearly 100 kinds of penstemons at plant sales during that same period of time. Further, the genus *Delosperma* and the spectacular southwestern *Agastache* (both major horticultural crops today that are grown and sold by the million around the world each year) can really be said to have had DBG as their horticultural birthplace. A tremendous number of plants in Front Range gardens and nurseries were originally displayed and often disseminated by DBG.

Over the last three decades, DBG staff have conducted dozens of focused collecting trips throughout the American West, from Alaska to New Mexico, obtaining over a thousand collections of native grasses, trees, shrubs, and wildflowers to be tested and displayed in DBG's many new native gardens. The first outstanding display of hardy manzanita outside the West Coast was assembled in the early 1980s at DBG, as well as a wealth of little-known woody plants, such as many rare western oaks, and obscure western shrubs, such as the silver-leaved barberries (*Mahonia*

haematocarpa, *M. fremontii*). Novel grasses such as prairie dropseed (*Blepharoneuron tricholepis*), giant sacaton (*Sporobolus wrightii*), and southwestern muhlenbergias were collected in the wild by DBG's staff and displayed at the Gardens long before they were sold commercially. In addition to dozens of penstemons and buckwheats new to cultivation, DBG's staff sought out prairie zinnia (*Zinnia grandiflora*), winecups (*Callirhoe involucrata*), red birds in a tree (*Scrophularia macrantha*), and hummingbird trumpet (*Epilobium canum* subsp. *garrettii*) long before they became widespread garden plants. By testing and selecting superior forms of native plants—and especially by displaying them in a variety of highly artistic settings throughout the York Street site, Centennial Park, and Chatfield Arboretum—DBG has educated visitors on the variety and utility of low-water native plants that can be used in home garden settings.

The search for new plants extends to other continents. Since 1994, four DBG staff members have traveled to southern Africa on eight trips, bringing back seeds of more than 1,000 kinds of plants. These plants have resulted in the only South African garden in a cold winter climate, as well as dozens of spectacular plant introductions, including both the largest and smallest red hot poker in cultivation (*Kniphofia northiae* and *K. hirsuta*, respectively). Over 100 kinds of South African ice plants—primarily *Delosperma*, but many other genera as well—have come through at least one Denver winter, bringing great notoriety to Denver in horticultural circles (and making "hardy in Denver" something of a mantra in nursery catalogues).

The arena of plant collection possesses an aura of romanticism, and perhaps even danger. Plant collectors must face uncertain weather, political conditions, and sometimes hostile environments abroad. A huge increase in regulations both domestically and abroad has made plant collecting increasingly tedious

bureaucratically, and there are always other daunting tasks: How do you find outstanding plants? How do you identify them in the field? Will you find ripe seeds and, if so, can you clean them properly? When you transport the seeds home, will they germinate? If they do, will you bring the seedlings to maturity and, if you do, will they persist? Then there are the challenges of finding the right places to grow the plants to observe them and ultimately to test their garden utility and parameters. And then, how does one go about monitoring performance, building stocks of challenging new crops while conducting the myriad activities of budget and personnel management, marketing, documentation, and communication that public gardeners must face from day to day?

In recent years, DBG staff have traveled, studied, and collected in several dozen countries throughout Asia, Europe, and the Southern Hemisphere, focusing more and more on high-altitude steppe-climate plants that have potential as durable ornamentals in Colorado and the interior West. Many of these steppe-climate plants have never been cultivated before. Many more are not found in any other public garden in North America or Eurasia. Additionally, Plant Select has underwritten several expeditions to New Mexico, Utah, and within Colorado. Meticulous treatment by staff in DBG's Plant Propagation Department, working closely with the horticulturists and designers at DBG, have ensured that a large proportion of these introductions have made it over the numerous hurdles outlined above to ensure that literally hundreds of outstanding ornamentals will continue to feed the Plant Select pipeline for years to come.

Panayoti Kelaidis is director of outreach at Denver Botanic Gardens in Denver, Colorado.

The Birth of Plant Select from a Green Industry Perspective   *by Al Gerace*

Colorado and the Rocky Mountain West present a unique set of climatic and agronomic challenges to gardeners, farmers, city planners, commercial developers, and environmentalists alike. Our dry High Plains and subalpine climates have extreme conditions rarely found in traditional developed areas around the world. Settlers to our area brought plants indigenous to their homelands in the Midwest, Great Britain, Central Europe, the Mediterranean, Asia, and along the eastern seaboard. The trees, shrubs, perennials, and annuals introduced to this area came mainly from more-humid locations with richer soils and friendlier water sources. The development of our region and regions like it is historically recent. Not since ancient times has there been so much pressure to develop settlements under such adverse horticultural circumstances.

How did Plant Select happen and why in Colorado? By 1995, Denver Botanic Gardens (DBG), with its fifty years of plant collections, exploration, and cultivation, had become a treasure trove of tantalizing botanical novelties. Plants from all parts of the world were thriving and languishing in full public view with little or no special watering. Once a year, DBG would offer a smattering of the more unusual plants to local plant enthusiasts and the public at its spring plant sale. Quantities were extremely limited, as the Gardens depended upon limited greenhouse facilities or local relationships with plant hobbyists and a few retail nurseries.

During those same fifty years, the whole national and local garden center and bedding plant industry was developing. All-America Selections (AAS), an international plant-testing organization, introduced the first commercial annual and perennial F_1 hybrids in the late 1940s. The local industry started out in a world of open-pollinated seeds, which were sold to consumers in packets, to sow directly into their gardens. Perennials and winter-hardy annuals were dug up in clumps and transported in strawberry baskets. Over the decades, the industry developed container-grown hybrid plants and special clones, thanks to very sophisticated propagation techniques and production facilities. Because of its high light conditions and a semiarid climate, Colorado was, and continues to be, an ideal location in which to cultivate hardy plants in a lower-disease environment for export to more-humid and populated areas. If plants could survive in Colorado, they could survive anywhere.

The Front Range of Colorado is also blessed with access to pure, snow-fed water from the Rockies. This pure water is vital for healthy propagation. Use of cold water to cool greenhouses economically, achieved with swamp-cooler technology developed by Professor Bob Holley at Colorado State University (CSU) in the 1950s, greatly enhanced production conditions. Holley was also involved in culture indexing of the Colorado carnation, which led to improved techniques in vegetative plant propagation. This technique, combined with the state's abundant sunlight, allowed the Colorado carnation industry to become the largest-scale production area in the United States, peaking in 1974. Further, Holley was one of the founding fathers of PanAmerican Seed, along with Charlie Weddle and Claude Hope, who were prime developers of F_1 hybrid flower seed varieties and commercial production of hybrid seeds—all of which had their origins in Colorado and contributed to the growth and modernization of the industry worldwide.

Colorado's local horticulture has been driven from the outside, with little regard for what is suited to the local climate. Programs such as AAS had no trial sites in this region until 1991, the closest site being at Bluebird Nursery in eastern Nebraska, which receives 30 inches of annual precipitation compared to about 15 inches along the Front Range. Growers and retailers in the state were saddled with promoting new plants that had not been tried locally, which led to a great deal of frustration on the part of the gardening public and growers alike. It was necessary for Colorado's green industries to become a part of these evaluations and decision-making processes, thereby emphasizing the significance of this region's semiarid conditions. CSU instituted the first AAS display site in the 1970s under Dr. Ken Goldsberry. Denver Botanic Gardens became a display site in 1989 through implementation of a grant from the newly formed Garden Centers of Colorado. Welby Gardens became a display site in 1990 and a trial site in 1991, when I served as a judge. CSU became a trial site in 1999, with Dr. James Klett as a judge.

Over these past fifty years, there has been much interplay between the local green industry, CSU, and DBG. CSU was a prime catalyst in the development of local grower and retail organizations, including the Carnation Co-op and associations such as the Colorado Flower Growers Association, Colorado Bedding and Pot Plant Association, Colorado Greenhouse Growers Association (CGGA), Garden Centers of Colorado, and the more recent merger of the CGGA and the Colorado Nursery Association into the Colorado Nursery and Greenhouse Association. The close collaboration between growers and the university led to a uniquely open grower-to-grower relationship. However, the decline of the local carnation industry led many growers to seek other growing and retail enterprises. A number of them opened garden centers and retail nurseries, while others established themselves as regional and national propagators of annuals and perennials for the burgeoning bedding plant industry. The whole industry was in search of the next stage of the green revolution and its very own market niche. During this time, the annual trial grounds at CSU were reinvigorated under the direction of Dr. Klett, with full participation of the local bedding plant industry.

Turkish veronica.

capture the imagination of the gardening public, but to keep their attention plant breeders needed to continually raise the standards of new introductions and legitimize their findings through rigorous trials and testing. This method was embodied in the AAS program. AAS gave the seed industry a way to focus attention on a limited number of new introductions, a method to ensure adequate supplies for broad-based promotion, and a means to spotlight the best of the best. It also served to financially reward those firms that were the best at innovation and production and yet were willing to share the profits with their colleagues through AAS for future promotion of new varieties.

The other half of the spark came in the mid-1990s, when DBG was also in search of ways to incorporate the evolution of new varieties and the revolution in vegetative, clonally propagated perennials and annuals into its garden designs. DBG's Plant Collections Committee sought to engage local green industry expertise to enhance DBG's already hefty horticultural presence. Representatives from local woody (tree and shrub) producers, retail garden center perennial professionals, young-plant propagators, an internationally recognized flower seed producer, and wholesale bedding plant growers sat down together with members of DBG staff and board of trustees to exchange and assimilate plant and flower knowledge for the growing palette of plants becoming available to gardeners around the world. Thanks to the participation of the local industry, outside members to this new group rediscovered the extensive endowment amassed at DBG over the decades. DBG, through their seed and plant exchange with other institutes and plant lovers from all over the world, as well as from plant exploration trips, now possessed hundreds of plants that could be made commercially available to the public. The Gardens' foremost spokesman for this fabulous collection was Panayoti Kelaidis, who at the time was curator of the Rock Alpine Garden and an avid collector of unusual plants for more than twenty years.

The stage was set with a botanical garden (DBG) laden with past riches and reaching out for the new wealth of modern horticulture; a state university (CSU) with a long-standing relationship with the green industry, a connection to the public through statewide extension services based on science, and the capability to provide the organizational discipline to set the group down its historical path; and a green industry fully developed with sophisticated production and propagation facilities. The industry, only recently armed with the technology of refined seed and vegetative young plants from clean cuttings, was ready to take a bold new marketing step. Because of the growth of local greenhouse, nursery, and garden center associations, all growers and retailers were now interacting on many levels and ready for innovation and discovery. With years of organizational development and local collaboration, growers and propagators were now ready to market directly to local allied independent retailers throughout the region.

Now put a few highly motivated plant lovers together, all with a vision of expanding a very restricted plant palette for the betterment of an entire region, and something was bound to happen. And it did. The botanical sparks from DBG catalyzed the plant-production machinery and sales potential of the local green industry to produce and sell in excess of 5 million Plant Select plants in just ten years. This triumverate of expertise (CSU, DBG, and the green industry) has proven to be a successful team focused upon satisfying the burgeoning demand from the gardening community for unique plants for their gardens. The proven success of the Plant Select plants now causes gardeners to specifically seek them out at garden centers. And, the green industry is committed to produce and provide them to gardeners in the Rocky Mountain West and beyond.

Al Gerace is CEO of Welby Gardens Company Inc. in Denver, Colorado.

The Jump-starting of Plant Select

Nearly twenty years ago, CSU and DBG drafted a memorandum of agreement for plant introduction and research. Gayle Weinstein and subsequently James E. Henrich at DBG, James E. Klett at CSU, and numerous other staff members of both institutions, along with prominent green industry professionals, spent countless hours debating and drafting academic protocols. A mission statement and goals, procedures, and protocols were also drafted.

If you had read the initial documents of Plant Select, you would have seen the broad outlines of the organization that exists today. It is a product of innumerable hours of debate, deep academic discussion, and numerous revisions. Plant Select started in the library and living plant museum of DBG and in the meeting rooms of DBG and CSU. The originators were charged with the tedious process of introducing and recommending new and better plants to the Rocky Mountain and Great Plains region.

The real spark that ignited Plant Select came simultaneously out of both right and left field. From the right, the spark came from the world of hybrid seed and plant production, a tradition no less noble in its rigor or in its mission than educational institutions, but rooted in the success or failure of the marketplace and ultimately on consumer acceptance. The competitive world of plant breeding had long before learned to

Plant Select Plants: Garden Design Considerations

by Dan Johnson

COMANCHE gooseberry.

Plant Select plants are chosen especially for adaptability in the Rocky Mountains and High Plains region, so how they are used in the landscape does not need to be rocket science. They are just one component of the broad palette of plants now available for use in our demanding climate. Whether you combine them with other plants for a long season of bloom, contrasting color or texture, or drought tolerance, all of the basic tenets of landscape design still apply. Like most good garden plants, once you consider water needs and season of bloom, combinations are entirely subjective, but some really stand out as new classic combinations for our western gardens and beyond.

The following are a few creative suggestions to take some of the mystery out of the process and make these plants even more user-friendly in your garden.

KINTZLEY'S GHOST honeysuckle.

SPANISH PEAKS foxglove.

- So far, many of the trees and shrubs in Plant Select have a common theme: **white or soft pastel flowers**. Use these to best advantage against a dark or evergreen backdrop, since they fade out against the open sky or pale buildings.

- Combine plants with a **hint of pink** (Carol Mackie daphne, CLEAR CREEK golden yellowhorn) with burgundy foliage or deeper pink flowers (redbud, roses) to enhance the pink shades.

- **Broadleaf evergreens**, such as manzanitas and mountain lover, provide restful neutral spaces in the garden. Larger ones, such as Alleghany viburnum, add texture all year and act as a dark backdrop for other flowering plants.

- Several shrubs can thrive with **little or no additional water** once established, including Apache plume, bluestem joint fir, fernbush, Mojave sage, wild thing sage, Furman's Red sage, PANCHITO manzanita, and SPANISH GOLD broom.

- Several perennials can thrive with **very little supplemental water** once established, including SILVER BLADE evening primrose, giant sacaton, Bridges' penstemon, Sea Foam artemisia, winecups, KANNAH CREEK buckwheat, TANAGER gazania, COLORADO GOLD gazania, SUNSET foxglove, and CRYSTAL RIVER veronica.

- **SPANISH GOLD broom** has a year-round texture similar to our native ephedras and looks great in naturalistic or desert-style landscapes. The golden spring flowers also combine especially well with blue or silver foliage (try bluestem joint fir); coarse textures of cacti, yucca, or agave; California poppies; or colorful mid-spring bulbs.

SILVERTON bluemat penstemon.

Turkish veronica.

PRAIRIE JEWEL penstemon and roses.

- Many of our perennials have **Western native** origins, either desert, mountain, or prairie. Consider their origins and that they are likely to combine easily in similar naturalistic landscapes with other native plants.

- **Backlighting** can enhance the color and texture of some plants. The fluffy seeds of Apache plume, bright scarlet-red seeds of HOT WINGS Tatarian maple, fiery red flowers of VERMILION BLUFFS Mexican sage, and waving plumes of giant sacaton will glow in the low light of morning or afternoon sun.

- **Apache plume** and bluestem joint fir are especially good in dry areas. Too much water can encourage plants to expand well beyond their original planting space, so plan accordingly.

- Use **silver foliage** (Sea Foam artemisia, silver sage, bluestem joint fir, silver dollar plant) to set off flowering plants or to allow neutral transitions in changing color schemes. Combine them with yellow or lime-green foliage and flowers for a fresh, sun-drenched look.

- Some are especially suited for use as an **edging or between pavers** with annuals such as alyssum and California poppy or other groundcovers such as thyme and snow-in-summer. These include Corsican violet, Turkish veronica, CRYSTAL RIVER veronica, SNOWMASS phlox, TANAGER gazania, COLORADO GOLD gazania, all ice plants, PLATINUM sage, and KANNAH CREEK buckwheat.

- Several plants can **reseed readily**, especially if grown with fine pea-gravel mulch. If older plants decline, new ones usually come along to replace them. These include DENVER GOLD columbine, winecups, TANAGER gazania, COLORADO GOLD gazania, SILVER BLADE evening primrose, silver sage, Furman's Red sage, Mojave sage, Corsican violet, and PRAIRIE JEWEL penstemon.

- **Hot flower colors** (found in such plants as Furman's Red sage, wild thing sage, winecups, ORANGE CARPET hummingbird trumpet, VERMILION BLUFFS Mexican sage, all of the ice plants, and gazanias) combine well with silver, lime-green, or gold foliage, but not always with each other. They also look great with purple, blue, or white flowers. Masses of simple combinations create the most impact.

- Plants with **unique colors**, such as CORAL CANYON twinspur or MESA VERDE ice plant, need just the right companions. Try silver, lime-green, or gold foliage, purple or white flowers, or ornamental grasses, yuccas, or cacti.

Winecups.

Vermilion Bluffs Mexican sage.

Snowmass phlox and tulips.

- Some plants have a **spreading or cascading** habit and are well suited to raised plantings, garden walls, or rock gardens. These include mock bearberry manzanita, Sea Foam artemisia, all of the ice plants, Silver Blade evening primrose, hopflower oregano, Pawnee Buttes sand cherry, Crystal River veronica, and winecups.

- For relatively **dry partial shade**, try Denver Gold columbine, mock bearberry manzanita, or Carol Mackie daphne.

- Perennials such as Remembrance columbine, Red Rocks penstemon, First Love dianthus, and cashmere sage do best in average soil with **moderate moisture**.

- **Hummingbirds** find the blooms of Bridges' penstemon, Vermilion Bluffs Mexican sage, agastaches, and Orange Carpet hummingbird trumpet irresistible. Plant them where you can enjoy the show.

- Site **fragrant plants**, such as Carol Mackie daphne, chocolate flower, and First Love dianthus, where the scent can be enjoyed: near a patio, doorway, or open window.

- Agastaches also create **smoldering combinations** with Russian sage, lavenders, purple smokebush, kniphofias, Mexican feather grass, blue oat grass, Indian Chief sedum, and *Verbena bonariensis*.

- All **agastaches** combine well with large rocks and heavily textured plants such as hardy cacti, agaves, or yuccas.

- Many early **bulbs** (alliums, crocus, species tulips) will grow through these same low plants and flower early, then disappear before the perennials put on their spring and summer displays.

Use these plants in imaginative and creative ways. Above all, enjoy them in your garden!

Dan Johnson is curator of native plants at Denver Botanic Gardens in Denver, Colorado.

How to Use This Book

Durable Plants for the Garden: A Plant Select Guide is a documentary publication featuring the first seventy-four plants promoted by Plant Select. Each of the plants is resilient and versatile, equally at home in a private garden or commercial landscape. Use *Durable Plants for the Garden* as a reference for program history, landscape design tips, and profiles on each plant. Each plant profile contains nomenclature, publication citation of the source species, lore that led to the plant's inclusion in the program, landscape design recommendations, descriptive characteristics of the plant, cultural requirements, and more. A six-foot-tall gardener figure is included for scale.

Use the provenance or nativity information (distribution, habitat, and elevation range) in each plant profile as a guide to the kind of environment to which the featured plant is most likely adapted. The native habitat elevation range should not be translated literally to your geographical locality. Why? Because the ranges encompass the extremes from both north and south latitudes: high elevation at southern latitudes may very well have higher annual mean temperature than that same elevation in northern latitudes. For this same reason you will see differences between the ranges in the native range of species and those found in the culture category. There is no direct correlation or formula that can be used to translate elevation into a hardiness zone.

As you peruse this book, you will see several kinds of names associated with each featured plant. Each has a specific purpose and meaning. The scientific name is the one true name that is specific to each plant, based primarily on floral and vegetative morphology, additional genetic characters, and established relationships to other plants. It is customary to italicize the scientific names, as in this example: *Oenothera* (the genus name) *macrocarpa* (species name) subsp. *incana* (a subspecies name). The names or abbreviated names associated with the scientific name commemorate the person or persons who discovered or studied the plant and originally made the name combination. For example, the *L.* associated with *Acer tataricum* stands for "Linnaeus," the author of this name combination and the father of the binomial (two-word) system of naming plants and animals. And the publication citation gives you the reference information for the original description of the plant.

In this publication, several other names are associated with each plant. A true common name can actually be used for or applied to completely unrelated plants, as it is the most common of names. "Grass" is a very broad-based common name that is often used to describe anything that is not a broad-leaved plant. "Beard tongue" is a common name used to describe all of the *Penstemon* species. Add a cultivar name to the scientific name and it becomes specific for all plants of that cultivated variety, such as "Princess Kay plum" for *Prunus nigra* 'Princess Kay'. Many of the Plant Select plants have a trademarked or registered trademark name, which is indicated in this book with capital letters, for example Vermilion Bluffs Mexican sage. Each of these names is most specifically associated with the original owner or developer of the plant and is used as a marketing tool. It is the link between, say, Plant Select and a particular plant such as Hot Wings Tatarian maple for *Acer tataricum* 'GarAnn' [PP15,023]. Throughout this book, the words of the registered and trademark names will appear without the accompanying ™ or ® symbols to distinguish them from scientific, cultivar, and common names. They are not to be confused with or used interchangeably with a scientific or common name.

Three plants have an additional component associated with the name. *Acer tataricum* 'GarAnn' [PP15,023], *Agastache cana* 'Sinning' [PP13,673], and *Delosperma* 'Kelaidis' [PP13,876] each bear a superscript symbol comprised of *PP* for "plant patent" and a serial number that is registered with the US Patent and Trademark Office. A patent is granted for plants that bear a genotypic characteristic unique to the taxon, for example hardiness, compact growth habit, flower color, or size. Plant patents can also be used as a tool to regulate propagation and distribution of the plant.

In addition to the main chapters, don't overlook the information contained in the appendix. Use the plant characteristic tables for quick reference. The bibliography citations will lead you to detailed plant descriptions from floristic treatments from around the globe. The resources section provides practical horticultural references to related plants from various climates, but especially semiarid environments. Use the comprehensive glossary to familiarize yourself with new terms. Don't miss Plant Select's website outlined in the additional resources section. The site is always up-to-date with the most current information.

Look for more unique plant promotions from the Plant Select program in the coming years. I hope the information chronicled on the following pages will help you successfully cultivate these durable plants in your own garden.

Blue Velvet honeysuckle.

Trees, Shrubs, and Woody Vines

Clockwise from top left: Apache plume, waxflower, CLEAR CREEK golden yellowhorn, HOT WINGS Tatarian maple, HOT WINGS Tatarian maple.

Hot Wings Tatarian maple

Samaras lavishly cover the plant in midsummer.

Pronunciation: **AH-ser tah-TARE-ih-cum**

Family: **Aceraceae – maple family**

Type of Plant: **Large shrub or small tree**

Height: **15 to 18 feet**

Spread: **15 to 18 feet**

Published: *Species Plantarum* 2:
1054. 1753. (for the
species)

Year Introduced: **2007**

Why Chosen

This remarkable maple was discovered as a chance-seedling growing in the production fields of Fort Collins Wholesale Nursery (Colorado) in the early 1990s. For six weeks every summer the seedling stood out from all of the other Tatarian maples due to its breathtaking display of scarlet red samaras contrasting with the rich green foliage, giving it a "Christmas in July" appearance. Hot Wings Tatarian maple performs especially well in semiarid climates because its parents come from continental central Asia. Other worthy attributes include the sturdy branching, adaptability to alkaline soil, and long season of visual interest.

This small tree truly stands out in the garden.

Scarlet red samaras distinguish this tree from other Tatarian maples.

Landscape Use

Ideal as a small specimen tree, in small groupings; well suited for use in small garden areas, parking strips, as a street tree, or in planter boxes.

Form

Rounded, upright, and shapely, with strong branch unions, making it less prone to storm damage.

Native Range of Species

Southeastern Europe into western Asia; in sunny, dry situations, often as forest undergrowth, rarely as a solitary tree; introduced into cultivation in 1759.

Characteristics

Flowers: Greenish to yellowish white, borne in upright panicles with the leaves in April.
Leaves: Opposite, usually not lobed, blade 2 to 4 inches across, lustrous, dark green, turn from yellow to orange-red in fall, deciduous.
Stems: Slender, reddish brown to brown, dotted with lenticels.
Fruits: ¾- to 1-inch-long samaras, wings nearly parallel, brilliant red in color, beginning in July.

Culture

Exposure: Full sun to partial shade.
Soil: Garden loam.
Soil Moisture: Moderate watering.
Hardiness: USDA zones 4 to 10.
Elevation Range: Up to 7,000 feet.

Best Features

More tolerant of alkaline soils than many maples. Long season of visual interest. Samaras more brilliant red and coloring earlier than is typical for the species.

Miscellaneous

Propagation is done mostly by budding onto *Acer tataricum* understock; cuttings root somewhat successfully. Because it is a patented variety, it must be reproduced vegetatively.

Acer tataricum 'GarAnn' 15

Mock bearberry manzanita

Its evergreen, low-growing habit makes it an excellent, eye-appealing groundcover.

Pronunciation: **ark-toe-STAFF-ih-los col-uh-rod-oh-EN-sis**

Family: **Ericaceae – heath family**

Type of Plant: **Evergreen shrub**

Height: **10 to 15 inches**

Spread: **36 to 85 inches**

Year Recommended: **2005**

Why Chosen

The source germplasm for this plant was collected by Betsy Baldwin in the late 1980s from a thriving hybrid swarm thought to be descended from *Arctostaphylos patula* and *A. uva-ursi*, found on the Uncompaghre Plateau. Baldwin (Sun Chaser Natives and Specialty Plants, Platteville, Colorado) selected the mock bearberry clone for its upright foliage, low growth habit, and propagation qualities. The original plant was again observed at its native site in the summer of 2007, now with a spread of 7 feet. Although all *Arctostaphylos ×coloradoensis* receive more precipitation naturally in their high-elevation habitat, they are extremely tolerant of dry conditions, as is this clone.

Landscape Use

Well suited as an evergreen groundcover, low-growing shrub, for informal mass planting on south-facing banks and hillsides, in full sun to dappled shade.

Form

Low-growing, glossy-leaved groundcover shrub.

Native Range of Species

The Uncompahgre Plateau of western Colorado near Grand Junction; in decomposed granite soil; 9,000 feet.

Close examination reveals tiny urn-shaped flowers in late winter to early spring.

Characteristics

Flowers: Urn shaped, white to pale pink, in congested panicles, February to April.

Leaves: Alternate, obovate to nearly oblanceolate, leathery, to 1 inch long, evergreen, often turn rich reddish purple in the fall.

Stems: Twisted and "muscular," often forming an attractive burl, rooting where in contact with soil.

Bark: Smooth, cinnamon-red, exfoliating.

Fruits: Globose, small berries, red, September through October.

Culture

Exposure: Full sun to partial shade.

Soil: Well-drained garden loam or sandy soil.

Soil Moisture: Xeric once established.

Hardiness: USDA zones 4b to 8.

Elevation Range: Up to 9,000 feet.

Best Features

Year-round attractive habit. Attractive bell-shaped flowers in early spring. Extremely drought tolerant. Evergreen foliage. Smooth, cinnamon-red exfoliating bark. Makes a thick carpet that can actually suppress weeds. Requires very little moisture once established.

Disadvantages

Can be slow to establish: "The first year it sits, the second it walks, the third it lopes." As far as water needs go, for the first couple of years it will need supplemental water every seven to ten days throughout the growing season when there is no precipitation, and monthly during extended dry periods the rest of the year.

Miscellaneous

Use 3-inch cuttings of previous year's growth taken from February through early April to propagate this bearberry. Strip off the lower few leaves, dip in rooting compound, mist the cuttings, seal in a plastic bag, and refrigerate overnight. The next day, quick-dip in a hydrogen peroxide solution, stick in small pots filled with rooting medium composed of three parts perlite to one part peat, place on a 70°F heating mat, and mist intermittently. Inoculate soil with a commercially available beneficial fungus product and ectomycorrhizal fungi for bearberries according to package directions. Rooting will begin in about three weeks.

Previously listed as *Arctostaphylos nevadensis* A. Gray var. *coloradensis* (Rollins) H. D. Harr. by Plant Select.

Evergreen leaves and reddish stems make this plant a garden feature year-round.

Arctostaphylos ×coloradoensis
PANCHITO manzanita

PANCHITO manzanita is a little more mounded and slightly more open than mock bearberry.

Pronunciation: **ark-toe-STAFF-ih-los col-uh-rod-oh-EN-sis**

Family: **Ericaceae – heath family**

Type of Plant: **Evergreen shrub**

Height: **10 to 15 inches**

Spread: **12 to 24 inches**

Year Introduced: **2006**

Why Chosen

The source germplasm for this plant was collected by Dermod Downs in the early 1980s from a thriving hybrid swarm thought to be descended from *Arctostaphylos patula* and *A. uva-ursi*, found on the Uncompaghre Plateau. While working at Wing Walker Western Native Plants (Parker, Colorado), Downs selected this clone for its more upright growth habit, bright green, oval evergreen leaves, and propagation qualities. He named it after his son Panchito. Very few broadleaf evergreens are propagated and sold in Colorado nurseries. Even fewer of these are sun and drought tolerant, making this selection a sure winner for the dry landscape.

Landscape Use

Good for informal mass planting on south-facing banks and hillsides, in full sun to dappled shade.

Form

Evergreen subshrub that forms low-mounding, glossy-leaved shrub.

Native Range of Species

The Uncompahgre Plateau of western Colorado near Grand Junction; in decomposed granite soil; 9,000 feet.

White to pale pink flowers are a pleasant surprise early in the garden season.

Panchito manzanita is an excellent alternative to groundcover junipers.

Characteristics

Flowers: Urn shaped, white to pale pink, in congested panicles, February to April.
Leaves: Alternate, obovate to nearly oblanceolate, leathery, to 1 inch long, evergreen, often turn rich reddish purple in the fall.
Stems: Upright, arching, twisted, and "muscular," often forming an attractive burl.
Bark: Smooth, cinnamon-red, exfoliating.
Fruits: Globose, small berries, red, in September through October.

Culture

Exposure: Full sun to partial shade.
Soil: Well-drained loam or sandy soil.
Soil Moisture: Moderate watering to xeric, once established.
Hardiness: USDA zones 4b to 8.
Elevation Range: Up to 9,000 feet.

Best Features

Drought tolerant. Attractive year-round habit. Evergreen. Once established it will require very little moisture.

Disadvantages

Slow to establish. Plants require supplemental water every seven to ten days throughout the growing season when there is no precipitation, and monthly during extended dry periods the rest of the year for the first couple of years after planting.

Miscellaneous

Use 3-inch cuttings of previous year's growth taken from February through early April to propagate this bearberry. Strip off the lower few leaves, dip in rooting compound, mist the cuttings, seal in a plastic bag, and refrigerate overnight. The next day, quick-dip in a hydrogen peroxide solution, stick in small pots filled with rooting medium composed of three parts perlite to one part peat, place on a 70°F heating mat, and mist intermittently. Inoculate soil with a commercially available beneficial fungus product and ectomycorrhizal fungi for bearberries according to package directions. Rooting will begin in about three weeks.

Arctostaphylos ×coloradoensis 19

Buddleja alternifolia Maxim. 'Argentea'
Silver fountain butterfly bush

Few shrubs produce such a festive shower of blooms.

Pronunciation: **BUD-lee-ah al-ter-neh-FOE-lee-ah**

Family: **Loganiaceae – logania family**

Type of Plant: **Large shrub or small tree**

Height: **12 to 15 feet**

Spread: **10 to 12 feet**

Published: *Bulletin de l'Académie Imperiale des Sciences de Saint-Pétersbourg* 26: 494. 1880. (for the species)

Year Recommended: **1998**

Why Chosen

The extravagant weeping stems of this large shrub are heavenly in late spring when draped with their bright lavender-blue flowers. One thing to remember is that flowers are produced only on old wood; heavy pruning will eliminate next year's flowers. This is the only butterfly bush that is reliably shrubby in much of the continental United States. With time, it can even be pruned to form a small tree. The 'Argentea' clone is not only much more silvery and attractive in leaf, but has proven to be at least one USDA plant hardiness zone hardier.

Leave plenty of room for this plant to adequately display its flowers and form.

Landscape Use

Integrates beautifully in shrub borders, as a specimen in a mixed border or lawn setting, or as an informal hedge.

Form

Long, slender stems give the plant a soft spreading and pendulous mounding habit.

Native Range of Species

Central and east central China; in thickets on riverbanks and along dry riverbeds; 4,900 to 13,100 feet.

Characteristics

Flowers: Tubular, lavender-blue to violet or purple with orange throat, fragrant, small, in terminal racemes, late spring.

Leaves: Alternate (atypical for genus and family), narrowly elliptic to nearly linear, to 4 inches long, covered densely with woolly hairs, deciduous.

Stems: Gracefully upright and arching.

Bark: Becoming corky and shreddy with age.

Fruits: Small, elliptic capsules.

Culture

Exposure: Full sun to partial shade.

Soil: Tolerates most soils.

Soil Moisture: Moderate watering.

Hardiness: USDA zones 4 to 8.

Elevation Range: Up to 8,000 feet.

Best Features

Has a measure of drought and cold tolerance. Thrives in a variety of sites and soils. Flowers early in the growing season.

A young silver fountain butterfly bush emerges among foxtail lilies and iris.

Disadvantages

Intolerant of excessive soil moisture.

Miscellaneous

This plant is rooted from semi-hardwood cuttings taken from May through mid-June. Silver fountain butterfly bush can be layered as well; dig up rooted layers before plants break dormancy in spring.

Buddleja alternifolia 'Argentea' 21

Chamaebatiaria millefolium Maxim.
Fernbush

Fernbush flowers are present throughout most of the summer.

Pronunciation: **kam-ee-bah-tee-AIR-ee-ah mil-le-FOE-lee-um**

Family: **Rosaceae – rose family**

Type of Plant: **Shrub**

Height: **3 to 5 feet**

Spread: **3 to 5 feet**

Published: ***Trudy Imperatorskago Saint-Petersburgskago Botaničeskago Sada* 6(1): 225. 1879.**

Year Recommended: **2006**

Why Chosen

Fernbush, one of the Southwest's greatest plant treasures, is named for its beautiful, deeply cut, fernlike leaves. The foliage is pleasantly aromatic when you brush against the plant or are pruning it back. Upright panicles of small white flowers resembling single roses cover the plant beginning in mid-June and often last into August. Mature stems exhibit a cinnamon-colored sheen, adding yet another attractive feature. Foliate buds give fernbush the appearance of being an evergreen shrub in the winter. Seed heads can be left through the winter for architectural interest. Once established in the garden, it is an extremely low-water-usage plant.

Desert-hardy companion plants such as rabbitbrush and cactus indicate the drought tolerance of fernbush.

Flowers are most spectacular when they first emerge at the beginning of summer.

Landscape Use

Ideal for shrub borders, informal hedges, or as a shrub specimen in mixed xeriscape borders. Combines well with other western natives and ornamental grasses. It may also be planted as a hedge border in challenging dry areas.

Form

Densely branched, stout shrub.

Native Range of Species

Oregon, Idaho, Wyoming, and south to California and Arizona; on basalt, limestone, and sandstone; often in piñon-juniper and spruce-fir communities; 4,500 to 8,000 feet.

Characteristics

Flowers: White flowers, to ⅔ inch across on upright panicles, mid-June to August.
Leaves: Alternate, much dissected (fernlike), covered with silvery soft, silky hairs, aromatic, sticky, semi-deciduous.
Bark: Shiny, reddish.
Fruits: Dry follicles, brown.

Culture

Exposure: Full sun to partial shade.
Soil: Garden loam, clay, or sandy soil.
Soil Moisture: Moderate watering, xeric once established.
Hardiness: USDA zones 4b to 8.
Elevation Range: Up to 7,000 feet.

Best Features

Tolerates shearing and pruning; best done annually in early winter. Needs no supplemental irrigation once established. Aromatic foliage. Large leaflike buds along the stems make it appear evergreen in winter.

Disadvantages

Fernbush is a forage crop for deer, sheep, goats, and other herbivores.

Miscellaneous

The seeds are miniscule and virtually impossible to distinguish from the chaff; germinates well with only a light cover of planting medium over the seeds.

Tea made from the leaves is used by Native Americans to settle upset stomachs and alleviate cramps.

Provides cover for small birds and mammals. Somewhat useful for erosion control.

Chamaebatiaria millefolium   23

Cytisus purgans (L.) Spach
SPANISH GOLD broom

A showy spring flower display belies the hardiness of this midsized shrub.

Pronunciation: **sigh-TIS-us PUR-gans**

Family: **Fabaceae — bean family**

Type of Plant: **Shrub**

Height: **4 to 6 feet**

Spread: **4 to 6 feet**

Published: ***Annales des Sciences Naturelles;
Botanique. Série 3. 3: 156. 1845.***

Year Introduced: **2000**

Why Chosen

One selection criterion for the plant palette of the Rock Alpine Garden at Denver Botanic Gardens (DBG) is acquisition of species with documented high-elevation provenance data. Plants of this subalpine shrub from the mountains of Spain, grown at DBG from seeds acquired from the University of Domaine Botanical Garden, were first planted in 1983. The bright golden yellow pealike flowers have an intense vanilla fragrance and are borne singly or paired from the leaf axils. Its nearly leafless, dull gray-green stems naturally form a low mound. SPANISH GOLD broom's tolerance of alkaline soil, heat, drought, and cold are additional desirable traits.

Landscape Use

Good for massing, as a specimen plant, foundation plant, or background border plant; effective among rocks and boulders; habitat for wildlife.

Form

A dense spreading mound of upright evergreen stems.

Native Range of Species

Mountains of central and southern France, west to Spain and eastern Portugal, south to Morocco; on dry, stony limestone slopes; 1,950 to 8,000 feet.

Characteristics

Flowers: Pealike, bright golden yellow, to ½ inch across, with intense vanilla fragrance, mid- to late spring.
Leaves: Alternate, oblanceolate, to ½ inch long, held close to the stem, covered with tiny, silky hairs, often early deciduous.
Stems: Dull grayish green, narrow, maintain color year-round.
Fruits: Small, flat legumes, to 1¼ inches long, blackish with three to six chestnut brown to blackish seeds.

Culture

Exposure: Full sun to partial shade.
Soil: Loam, clay loam, or gravelly soils.
Soil Moisture: Average, not too wet.
Hardiness: USDA zones 4a to 9.
Elevation Range: Up to 8,000 feet.

Best Features

Better adapted to regional growing conditions than the selections and hybrids of Scotch broom (*Cytisus scoparius*). The prodigious display of flowers is unaffected by extremes of weather. Extremely tolerant of drought and alkaline soils.

Left: SPANISH GOLD broom makes an outstanding specimen plant.

Right: The evergreen stems make this a plant of interest throughout the year.

Disadvantages

Intolerant of poorly drained, wet soils.

Miscellaneous

Cuttings are rooted from semi-hardwood stock in May to June; they must be kept moderately dry or they will rot.

Cytisus purgans   25

Carol Mackie daphne

Not only are Carol Mackie daphne's early spring flowers appealing, so is their intense fragrance.

Pronunciation: **DAPH-knee burk-WOOD-ee-eye**

Family: **Thymelaeaceae – mezereum family**

Type of Plant: **Deciduous shrub**

Height: **3 to 4 feet**

Spread: **3 to 4 feet**

Published: *Arnoldia* **30(6): 253. 1970.**

Year Recommended: **1997**

Why Chosen

Carol Mackie daphne is named for a keen gardener in Far Hills, New Jersey, who discovered this showy sport with cream-edged leaves in her garden. Cuttings were shared with Don and Hazel Smith of Watnong Nursery. The sport was so spectacular, it quickly found its way to Wayside Gardens in Hodges, South Carolina, which promoted and distributed the hybrid nationwide.

Carol Mackie thrives in the alkaline soils of the Rocky Mountain region, quickly forming a symmetrical mound that is smothered with clusters of intensely fragrant white or pale pink flowers in late April and May, with occasional flushes into fall. The foliage often persists through much of the winter.

Carol Mackie daphne is a great companion to eastern redbud trees, miniature iris, and other early spring flowering plants.

Landscape Use

Ideal as an accent plant, focal point, specimen plant, in shrub borders, mixed borders, or as an informal hedge. Site plant to allow access to the fragrant flowers.

Form

Densely branched, upright low-mounding shrub.

Native Range of Species

The Burkwood daphnes resulted from a cross between *Daphne caucasica* and *D. cneorum*; the former is found in the Caucasus Mountains and the latter is native in Europe, from Spain to southwestern Russia.

Characteristics

Flowers: Tubular, flared, small, white flushed with pink, fragrant, early to mid-spring.

Leaves: Alternate, simple, linear-oblanceolate or narrowly elliptic oblanceolate, to 1¼ inches long, cream-edged green leaves, somewhat persistent.

Stems: Upright, densely branched.

Bark: Smooth, gray.

Fruits: Small drupes.

Culture

Exposure: Sun or partial shade.

Soil: Loam; does not respond well to heavy fertilization.

Soil Moisture: Moderate watering.

Hardiness: USDA zones 4a to 9.

Elevation Range: Up to 9,000 feet.

Best Features

Leaves more or less persistent into winter. Fragrant flowers. Cold tolerant and tolerant of alkaline soils. Readily forms extremely symmetrical mounding shape.

Disadvantages

Not known to be long-lived. Seeds are toxic if ingested. Heavy layers of snow can disfigure the mounded form; gently shake or brush snow from branches as soon as possible after snowfall.

Miscellaneous

This is probably the easiest of all the daphnes to root. Cuttings can be taken any time the plants are actively growing but not flowering. If the stems get very woody, just wound them to allow new roots to emerge from the outer cambium layer.

Ephedra equisetina Bunge
Bluestem joint fir

Bluestem joint fir provides a soft texture to an otherwise prickly-textured dry garden.

Pronunciation: **ee-FED-rah EH-qui-seh-tee-nah**

Family: **Ephedraceae – Mormon tea or joint fir family**

Type of Plant: **Evergreen shrub**

Height: **4 to 6 feet**

Spread: **3 to 8 feet**

Published: ***Mémoires de l'Académie Imperiale des Sciences de Saint-Pétersbourg. Sixieme Série. Mathématiques, Physiques et Naturelles 7: 501. 1851.***

Year Introduced: **2004**

Why Chosen

Denver Botanic Gardens acquired seeds of bluestem joint fir from the botanical garden of the University of Coimbra (Coimbra, Portugal) in 1984. This gymnosperm was selected because it performs well in arid, alkaline conditions like those in the Front Range of Colorado. Fort Collins Wholesale Nursery realized the ornamental value of this plant and began production on a limited basis in 1998. Nondescript chartreuse cones appear like foam on the stems in April and May. However, female plants bear bright red berrylike cones (naked seeds surrounded by a fleshy outer layer) that ripen in midsummer, providing a pleasing accent to the leafless bluish gray-green stems.

Landscape Use

Well suited for massing, as a specimen plant, foundation plant, or background plant in a border, rock garden, or among boulders; also nice in wildlife plantings.

Form

Stiff, narrow, evergreen, upright stems.

Native Range of Species

Ephedra equisetina is distributed from northern China to Inner Mongolia and the mountains of central and middle Asia; in dry and rocky places; 2,600 to 9,800 feet.

Bluestem joint fir (upper left) makes a substantial background plant to smaller plants.

Colorful berrylike cones appear on the stems of female plants in midsummer.

Characteristics

Flowers: Insignificant yellow pollen and seed cones, of little interest, in spring.
Leaves: Opposite, simple, brown, rudimentary.
Stems: Erect to procumbent, bluish gray-green, attractive throughout the year.
Fruits: Seed cones elongate-ovoid to ovoid, opposite at nodes, bright red and fleshy at maturity, about ⅓ inch in diameter, each bearing two seeds, maturing in midsummer on female plants.

Culture

Exposure: Full sun to partial shade.
Soil: Garden loam, clay, or sandy soil.
Soil Moisture: Moderate watering to xeric.
Hardiness: USDA zones 4b to 9.
Elevation Range: Up to 7,000 feet.

Best Features

Established plants are both drought resistant and lime tolerant. Performs well in full-sun to partial-shade exposures.

Disadvantages

Does not perform well in wet, poorly drained soils.

Miscellaneous

Depending on collection timing and environmental conditions, most seeds are hollow and nonviable, making seed collection and cleaning very laborious. Viable seeds sink in water and require at least a thirty-day cold stratification before sowing.

Ephedra has a more than 2,000-year history of use in China. Known there as *ma huang*, it has been used as a diuretic, a treatment for respiratory ailments, headaches, aching joints and bones, and edema, as well as a stimulant tea.

Mormon tea and joint fir are well known to botanists, but are perhaps most famous for the chemical compound they produce: ephedrine, one of nature's most potent stimulants and appetite suppressants.

Mature fleshy cones are quickly discovered and consumed by birds.

Fallugia paradoxa (D. Don) Endl. ex Torr.
Apache plume

Late spring brings on the first flush of roselike white flowers.

Pronunciation: **fahl-OO-gee-ah par-ah-DOCKS-ah**

Family: **Rosaceae – rose family**

Type of Plant: **Deciduous shrub**

Height: **4 to 6 feet**

Spread: **4 to 6 feet**

Published: ***Notes of a Military Reconnoissance*** 139. 1848.

Year Recommended: **2002**

Why Chosen

This glorious shrub, native to the Southwest, is a member of the rose family and has long been offered in the Colorado nursery trade but has never been grown as widely as deserved. Delicate, brilliant white to pale pink flowers similar to small single roses are produced throughout the summer on this durable, fine-textured shrub. The feathery pink styles are persistent, providing a dramatic second act as the wonderfully showy, shimmering tassels last into the winter. The flowers and tassels are often present simultaneously, adding to the ornamental value, especially when backlit by the sun. Apache plume is extremely hardy, adaptable, and able to withstand prolonged dry conditions.

Left and middle: By midsummer, flowers continue sporadically, but each leaves long-lasting, feathery, cream to pink styles, which can completely cover the plant. Right: Winter texture is light and airy.

Landscape Use

Ideal as an accent plant or in small groupings in dry areas of the garden, as the background of the perennial border, and in native landscape designs.

Form

Rounded, fine-textured shrub.

Native Range of Species

Utah south to Texas, west to California, and south into north-central Mexico; on rocky slopes and in washes; 3,500 to 8,000 feet.

Characteristics

Flowers: Roselike, solitary on long stalks, white, 1½ inches across, May to September.
Leaves: Alternate, wedge shaped, pinnately divided into three to seven narrow lobes, nearly evergreen, rusty-scaly beneath, persisting into the winter.
Stems: Covered with short, soft hairs when young.
Bark: Whitish to straw-colored, exfoliating.
Fruits: Achene with pinkish persistent style, to 1½ inches long, persistent from summer into winter.

Culture

Exposure: Full sun to partial shade.
Soil: Sandy soil or clay loam; not particular.
Soil Moisture: Moderate watering to dry.
Hardiness: USDA zones 4 to 8.
Elevation Range: Up to 7,000 feet

Best Features

Apache plume is extremely useful for sunny, hot, and dry locations. It has proven to be somewhat resistant to browsing by deer. Flowers are produced from spring to frost, on shrubs that have an attractive, rounded habit. Needs little supplemental water once established.

Miscellaneous

Seeds that are fresh, even a little green, germinate within days of being sown. Older seeds have physiological dormancies that are challenging to overcome.

Useful for wildlife cover and forage.

Fallugia is monotypic but will hybridize with *Purshia tridentata* (antelope bush).

Various preparations or parts of the plant have been used by Native Americans as a ceremonial emetic, to promote hair growth, and to make rough brooms, baskets, cradleboards, and arrows.

Jamesia americana Torr. & A. Gray
Waxflower

Pronunciation: **JAMES-ee-ah ah-mer-ah-CANE-ah**

Family: **Hydrangeaceae – hydrangea family**

Type of Plant: **Deciduous shrub**

Height: **3 to 6 feet**

Spread: **4 to 6 feet**

Published: *A Flora of North America* 1(4): 593–594. 1840.

Year Recommended: **2003**

Why Chosen

Jamesia commemorates its collector, Edwin James, botanist for the Long Expedition, which surveyed the Front Range in 1820. Its common name refers to the unique waxy white flowers that are quite fragrant and resemble orange blossoms in appearance. The flowers are held above leaves that are heavily textured, deep green above, and covered with soft white hairs beneath. Waxflower also has great color in fall, when it takes on rich pink and orange tints. Silvery, reddish brown peeling bark gives it a handsome winter appearance. In addition to the attractive flowers, foliage, and growth habit, this native beauty is quite drought tolerant and especially useful for drier shaded areas.

Landscape Use

Ideal as a specimen, accent, grouping in the back of perennial borders, foundation plant, among boulders or in crevices, in naturalistic landscapes; position so the reddish brown bark is visible in winter.

Form

Densely branched, naturally mounding shrub.

Native Range of Species

Wyoming and Utah to New Mexico, Arizona, and into Sierra Nevada of California; on the walls of canyons, slopes, cliffs, crevices, in coniferous forests; 7,500 to 9,500 feet.

Heavily textured bright green leaves form a contrasting background for late spring flowers. As shown here, waxflower performs well in partial shade.

Characteristics

Flowers: Waxy, five-petaled, white to pink, ½ to ¾ inch in diameter, numerous in dense cymes, lightly fragrant, May and June.
Leaves: Opposite, blades ovate, with shallowly round-toothed margins, bright green above, underside with soft white hairs, changing to pink and orange shades in fall, deciduous.
Stems: Rigid, upright, densely branched.
Bark: Reddish brown, exfoliating.
Fruits: Capsule to ³⁄₁₆ inch long, brown.

Culture

Exposure: Sun to partial shade.
Soil: Well-drained loam or gravelly soil.
Soil Moisture: Moderate watering to dry.
Hardiness: USDA zones 3 to 8.
Elevation Range: Up to 10,000 feet.

Best Features

Tolerates dry, shady conditions. Beautiful reddish brown peeling bark. Fragrant flowers. Bright green foliage that changes to pink and orange shades in fall.

Fall leaf color extends this plant's seasonal value in the garden.

Miscellaneous

These plants are easily grown from seeds, but using fresh seeds is crucial, as viability diminishes rapidly with age.

Lonicera korolkowii Stapf 'Floribunda'
Blue Velvet honeysuckle

An abundance of flowers adorn this shrub's handsome form in early spring.

Pronunciation: **lon-IH-sir-ah core-al-COW-ee-eye**

Family: **Caprifoliaceae – honeysuckle family**

Type of Plant: **Herbaceous shrub**

Height: **10 to 12 feet**

Spread: **6 to 8 feet**

Published: ***Garden & Forest*** **7: 34, fig. 4. 1894.**
(for the species, not the cultivar)

Year Introduced: **1999**

Why Chosen

Sutherland Nursery (Boulder, Colorado) sent the original plants of this variety to the Cheyenne Experiment Station (Cheyenne, Wyoming). This clone was subsequently selected from old plants that have persisted for decades in that region's harsh climate. The silvery blue foliage, which is persistent and attractive through the entire growing season, distinguishes it from the more common Tatarian honeysuckle. It is resistant to honeysuckle witches' broom aphids and the disfiguring growths that typically result from these infestations. This cultivar name references its more floriferous nature compared with the typical species. The species' name commemorates General N. J. Korolkov, a Russian botanist who collected plants in central Asia in the 1870s.

Long, arching branches appear to spray flowers in all directions. This mature specimen exceeds the plant spread typical for this cultivar but maintains the characteristic profusion of bloom.

Landscape Use

Excellent as a specimen for a small yard or background plant in large mixed border and for massing in large yards.

Form

Large, multistemmed shrub, stems arching and forming a vase-shaped silhouette.

Native Range of Species

Hindu Kush Mountains of northern Afghanistan and Pakistan, southern Tian Shan Mountains of Kazakhstan; 4,900 to 13,100 feet.

Characteristics

Flowers: Tubular, petal tips reflexed, to ⅔ inch long, borne in axillary pairs, soft pink, early spring.
Leaves: Opposite, ovate-elliptic, to about 1 inch long, pale bluish green, covered with short, soft hairs above and beneath, deciduous.
Stems: Upright to gently arching.
Bark: Exfoliating on mature stems.
Fruits: Berries, globose, bright red, maturing in midsummer.

Culture

Exposure: Full sun to partial shade.
Soil: Does best in sandy or clay loam.
Soil Moisture: Moderate watering to dry.
Hardiness: USDA zones 3 to 8.
Elevation Range: Up to 9,000 feet.

Best Features

Vase-shaped growth form, bluish green foliage. Tolerates a wide range of soils and sites. Resistant to honeysuckle witches' broom aphids.

Disadvantages

Establishes with more difficulty than other honeysuckles. Susceptible to powdery mildew.

Miscellaneous

Propagated from semi-hardwood cuttings taken from May through June. Stick cuttings in a sand frame or containers with a well-draining medium.

Lonicera prolifera (Kirchner) Rehder
KINTZLEY'S GHOST honeysuckle

White, nearly circular silver-dollar-sized bracts surrounding the stem just below the flowers persist into autumn.

Pronunciation: **lon-IH-sir-ah proh-LIF-ir-ah**

Family: **Caprifoliaceae – honeysuckle family**

Type of Plant: **Perennial woody vine**

Height: **8 to 12 feet**

Spread: **3 to 6 feet**

Published: *Rhodora* 12: 166. 1910.

Year Introduced: **2006**

Why Chosen

William P. "Ped" Kintzley, a gifted natural horticulturist who worked in the Iowa State University greenhouses (Ames, Iowa), selected this improved form of the species in the early 1880s. The plant, from which members of the Kintzley clan received propagules, grew on the graves of Ped's parents in Good Hope Cemetery near Cherokee, Iowa. Scott Skogerboe (Fort Collins Wholesale Nursery) found this unusual honeysuckle growing in the yard of grandson Lee Kintzley in north Fort Collins, Colorado, in 2001. The nearly tubular flowers, borne in several-flowered cymules, open pale yellow and fade to pale orange, followed by orange to red berries. The most dramatic feature of this species, however, is the persistent, white, nearly circular, silver-dollar-sized bract surrounding the stem just below the flowers, resembling silver dollar eucalyptus.

The woody vines can grow 8 to 12 feet.

Late spring flowers produce berries that change from yellow to bright red by midsummer.

Landscape Use

Excellent cover specimen to twine on fences, arbors, and pergolas.

Form

Twining woody vine.

Native Range of Species

Native in northeast and upper central United States from central New York, west to Wisconsin, and south to Missouri and Arkansas; in moist woods and thickets.

Characteristics

Flowers: Tubular, two-lipped, about 1 inch long, pale yellow fading to pale orange, hairy inside tube, paired three-flowered inflorescences borne terminally, June.

Leaves: Opposite, simple, lower broadly ovate, 1½ to 3½ inches long, upper two to four pairs somewhat to fully united at their bases and nearly spherical, long persistent, strikingly covered with a bloom that can be rubbed off above, without hairs beneath, deciduous.

Stems: Woody, climbing, without hairs.

Fruits: Berries, yellow changing to red and then bright red, midsummer to fall.

Culture

Exposure: Full sun to partial shade.
Soil: Garden loam.
Soil Moisture: Moderate watering.
Hardiness: USDA zones 4 to 8.
Elevation Range: Up to 8,000 feet.

Best Features

The most dramatic aspect of this species is the pure white, nearly circular, silver-dollar-sized bracts that surround the stem, just below the flowers, persisting into autumn.

Miscellaneous

Cuttings root easily from vegetative growth. Once the plants begin to flower, rooting percentages decrease greatly, so take the cuttings you need early.

Previously listed as *Lonicera reticulata* Champ. ex Benth. by Plant Select.

Paxistima canbyi A. Gray
Mountain lover

Mountain lover is one of the few plants that thrives in the dry shade of a conifer.

Pronunciation: **pax-IH-stih-mah CAN-bee-eye**

Family: **Celastraceae – bittersweet family**

Type of Plant: **Evergreen shrub**

Height: **8 to 12 inches**

Spread: **15 to 20 inches**

Published: ***Proceedings of the American Academy of Arts and Sciences* 8: 620. 1873.**

Year Recommended: **2003**

Why Chosen

This very local, mat-forming evergreen shrub is quite rare in the Allegheny Mountains of Pennsylvania and nearby states, where it is native. Like many rare plants, it seems to revel in cultivation, thriving especially well in that most challenging of garden environments: dry shade. Distantly related to *Euonymus*, this twiggy shrub likewise has inconspicuous flowers that do little to enhance its beauty. The genus name is derived from the Greek word *pachus*, meaning "thick," and *stigma*, describing its thick stigma. William Marriott Canby is commemorated in the species' name. An alternate common name is *rat stripper*, because these rodents are known to strip its bark for food in winter.

Small green flowers borne in early spring are nearly inconspicuous.

Lustrous, dark green evergreen foliage is the most noticeable trait of this plant, whereas the tiny fruits are nearly imperceptible.

Landscape Use

Ideal as a low hedge, foreground of the shade border, in informal plantings, woodland designs, and as groundcover.

Form

Twiggy, low-mounding shrub.

Native Range of Species

Allegheny Mountains of Virginia, West Virginia, Kentucky, into southern Ohio, Pennsylvania, Tennessee, and North Carolina; among calcareous rocks on slopes.

Characteristics

Flowers: Green petals, small and inconspicuous, April.
Leaves: Opposite, simple, linear-oblong, to 1 inch long, mostly entire to finely notched at the tips, leathery, leaf margins rolled under, lustrous dark green, evergreen with purple tints in winter.
Stems: Ascending to reclining with tips ascending, rooting where they contact the soil.
Fruits: Capsules, oblong, to 3/16 inch long, white, with basal multiple-lobed aril.

Culture

Exposure: Partial shade to shade.
Soil: Loamy soils are best.
Soil Moisture: Moderate watering.
Hardiness: USDA zones 4 to 9.
Elevation Range: Up to 7,000 feet.

Best Features

Tolerates alkaline soils and performs well in moist to dry shade. Very useful as an evergreen groundcover beneath large shrubs.

Disadvantages

Intolerant of foot traffic when grown as a groundcover. Slow rate of growth.

Miscellaneous

Propagate either from softwood or hardwood cuttings, although rooting success rate is low for each method. Stems can be layered in the garden.

Philadelphus lewisii Pursh
CHEYENNE mock orange

Stunning flowers typical of mock oranges are displayed on billowy branches of a comparatively compact shrub.

Pronunciation: **fill-ah-DEL-fuss lew-ISS-ee-eye**

Family: **Hydrangeaceae – hydrangea family**

Type of Plant: **Shrub**

Height: **6 to 8 feet**

Spread: **6 to 8 feet**

Published: *Flora Americae Septentrionalis* 1: 329. 1814.

Year Introduced: **2001**

Why Chosen

This mock orange is the state flower of Idaho. It can be found throughout the inland Pacific Northwest, often in semiarid canyons as well as along the margins of montane woodlands. This clone was selected at the USDA Cheyenne Horticultural Field Station (now named High Plains Arboretum), a satellite of the Cheyenne Botanic Gardens, where it has survived decades of harsh Great Plains winters without supplemental watering or care. Unlike the often gangly growth habit of typical mock oranges, the stems of this clone form a billowy, pleasing mound covered with dark blue-green foliage. The species' name commemorates Meriwether Lewis, who first collected it in 1806.

Flowers first appear in midspring, covering the shrub, and continue sporadically into midsummer.

Landscape Use

Ideal for naturalistic landscapes, mixed shrub plantings, background of perennial border, short- to midgrass meadows, foundation plantings, and woodland gardens; site for easy access to fragrant flowers.

Form

Erect, multibranched shrub that becomes somewhat vase shaped.

Native Range of Species

Northwestern North America from the Cascade Mountains eastward to Montana and Utah, south to California.

Characteristics

Flowers: Four-petaled in terminal racemes, to 2 inches across, white with prominent yellow stamens, with fragrance of citrus, May through July.
Leaves: Opposite, mostly ovate, entire to finely toothed, to 2¾ inches long, covered with short, soft hairs on veins beneath, dark blue-green, deciduous.
Stems: Erect, branched, somewhat arching.
Bark: Matures to a shiny cinnamon color.
Fruits: Capsules with many seeds.

Culture

Exposure: Full sun to partial shade.
Soil: Ordinary or sandy loam or dry clay.
Soil Moisture: Moderate watering to dry.
Hardiness: USDA zones 3 to 9.
Elevation Range: Up to 8,000 feet.

Best Features

Fragrant, large white flowers. Attractive cinnamon-colored bark.

Disadvantages

Requires periodic rejuvenation pruning to encourage new stems. Very sensitive to herbicides.

Miscellaneous

These plants can be grown from seeds or cuttings (softwood or semi-hardwood). Rooting medium needs to be well drained; set intermittent mist frequency just to sustain cuttings from wilting. For best germination, seeds should be cold stratified for eight weeks before sowing.

Used for erosion control and moderately important for animal forage.

Various preparations of the plant were used by Native Americans as cathartics, dermatological aids, or to make cradle hoops, snowshoes, fish spears, root diggers, baskets, arrows, and soap.

Prunus besseyi L. H. Bailey
PAWNEE BUTTES sand cherry

Flowers cover the stems of the sprawling PAWNEE BUTTES sand cherry around the first of May, as seen here during a spring rain.

Pronunciation: **PREW-nuss BES-see-eye**

Family: **Rosaceae – rose family**

Type of Plant: **Deciduous shrub**

Height: **15 to 18 inches**

Spread: **4 to 6 feet**

Published: *Bulletin of the Cornell Agricultural Experiment Station* **70: 261. 1894.**

Year Introduced: **2000**

Why Chosen

This compact, prostrate form of the normally upright sand cherry was collected as cuttings in 1983 by Jim Borland and Panayoti Kelaidis (Denver Botanic Gardens) on the slopes of the Pawnee Buttes in north-central Colorado. The fragrant ivory flowers are produced from late April into May, followed by a bounty of tasty cherries in midsummer. Its glossy, dark gray-green foliage is very attractive during the growing season and often turns a glowing red to maroon color in the autumn. In nature, this tough, matted shrub grows in harsh clay and endures drought and extreme environmental conditions. The Latin name commemorates Charles Edwin Bessey, an American professor of botany, pioneering ecologist, and student of Asa Gray.

Left: Summer leaf color.
Right: Fall leaf color.

Landscape Use

Nice as a small specimen or accent plant; excellent among rocks or sprawling over low walls, in naturalistic gardens, or on parking islands.

Form

Small shrub with spreading prostrate branches; stem tips often ascending.

Native Range of Species

Manitoba to Wyoming, south to Minnesota and Colorado; among tall grasses, barren sandy areas, or on rocky mesas; 3,500 to 6,500 feet.

Characteristics

Flowers: Five-petaled, to ½ inch across, white, in sessile umbels, produced in abundance, late April into May.
Leaves: Alternate, simple, oval-lanceolate, somewhat saw-toothed, to 2½ inches long, changing from gray-green to maroon-red in fall, deciduous.
Stems: Without hairs, erect to prostrate, often with ascending tips.
Bark: Reddish brown in color.
Fruits: Plum-shaped drupes, to ¾ inch long, blue-black, midsummer; edible, sweet.

Culture

Exposure: Full sun to partial shade.
Soil: Sandy soil or clay loam (not fussy).
Soil Moisture: Moderate watering to dry.
Hardiness: USDA zones 3 to 8.
Elevation Range: Up to 9,000 feet.

Best Features

Tolerates hot and dry conditions. Drought tolerant. Architectural branching habit. Maroon-red fall color.

Disadvantages

Does not perform well in poorly drained soil.

Miscellaneous

These plants can be propagated from semi-hardwood cuttings taken in early June, stem layering, root cuttings taken in winter, or from seeds that have been cold stratified for three to four months.

Plants provide food and cover for wildlife; good for revegetation and soil stabilizing; fresh or dried fruits can be used to make jams, jellies, or syrup.

Princess Kay plum

Princess Kay plum bears white, many-petaled flowers in profusion in spring.

Pronunciation: **PREW-nuss NYE-grah**

Family: **Rosaceae – rose family**

Type of Plant: **Deciduous tree**

Height: **15 to 20 feet**

Spread: **12 to 15 feet**

Published: ***Hortus Kewensis* 2: 165. 1789. (for the species, not the cultivar)**

Year Recommended: **2000**

Why Chosen

This variant of the typical species was found in the wild by Catherine and Robert Nyland in Itasca County, Minnesota. Introduced into cultivation by the Minnesota Landscape Arboretum, this white double-flowered form of *Prunus nigra* develops a neat, oval-shaped crown. Attractive green foliage follows, changing to spectacular shades of yellow, orange, and red in the fall. The dark brown bark is an additional handsome feature; it showcases the winter form and four-season appeal of this underused selection. Princess Kay plum is a relatively fast growing, small- to medium-sized flowering tree.

This tree's oval-shaped structure is visible in the winter.

Autumn color is as spectacular as the spring flower display.

Landscape Use

Small ornamental tree suitable for grouping in larger areas or as an individual specimen in smaller spaces.

Form

An oval-shaped crown spreads to about 15 feet.

Native Range of Species

Southern Quebec to Manitoba, south to Georgia and Louisiana.

Characteristics

Flowers: Many-petaled, to 1¼ inches across, white, borne in profusion in umbels, April to May.

Leaves: Alternate, elliptic to obovate, 2 to 4 inches long, simple, margins doubly saw-toothed, without hairs above, may be lightly covered with short, soft hairs beneath, dark green changing to shades of yellow, orange, or red in fall, deciduous.

Bark: Dark brown to nearly black, with prominent lenticels.

Fruits: Oval-shaped drupes, yellowish red to red, August.

Culture

Exposure: Sun to partial shade.
Soil: Ordinary garden loam.
Soil Moisture: Moderate watering.
Hardiness: USDA zones 4b to 9.
Elevation Range: Up to 7,000 feet.

Best Features

The tree flowers heavily even as a young plant, adding a bright note to the spring landscape. Features spectacular fall color ranging in shades of yellow, orange, and red. Dark-colored bark with prominent lenticels create winter interest.

Disadvantages

Flowers are short-lived. New growth is prone to aphid infestation, potentially causing deformation.

Miscellaneous

These plants are grown vegetatively. Plants are grafted as well as rooted from cuttings.

Native Americans used preparations from bark or roots as cough medicine and antiemetics, fruits for a variety of foodstuffs, and an infusion from the inner bark as a mordant.

Rhamnus smithii Greene
Smith's buckthorn

This handsome, dense, thornless shrub is an excellent screen or barrier between properties.

Pronunciation: **RAM-nus SMITH-ee-eye**

Family: **Rhamnaceae – buckthorn family**

Type of Plant: **Shrub**

Height: **8 to 10 feet**

Spread: **8 to 10 feet**

Published: *Pittonia* **3: 17. 1896.**

Year Recommended: **2002**

Why Chosen

Several decades ago, Smith's buckthorn caught the attention of George Kelly and Harry Swift, both pioneers in regional horticulture. They observed qualities in this plant that led to more than twenty years of evaluation at the Upper Colorado Plant Environment Center at Meeker. Sturdy, thornless branches exhibit an elegant, muscular form that supports dark green foliage embellished with black fruit beginning in late summer. Smith's buckthorn is tailor-made for attracting birds to the garden; they welcome the shelter and food provided by this handsome shrub.

Left: The pale yellowish green fall foliage brightens the landscape.

Right: The strong stem structure is revealed in its winter form.

Landscape Use

Suitable for screening, as a specimen plant, or as a windbreak. Dark green leaves are a beautiful contrast to lighter colored, softer textured plants.

Form

Densely branched, upright, symmetrical oval shape, to about 10 feet.

Native Range of Species

Colorado (southwestern and western) into New Mexico, but probably farther west; in valleys and on hillsides; about 7,000 feet.

Characteristics

Flowers: Four-petaled, greenish, nearly inconspicuous, unisexual, axillary, April to May.
Leaves: Alternate to subopposite, elliptic, serrulate, 1 to 2 inches long, green to yellowish green, paler below, glossy above, without hairs, deciduous.
Stems: Thornless, without hairs to covered with short, soft hairs, appearing "muscular."
Fruits: Berries, globose, to about ⅜ inch in diameter, black, late summer.

Culture

Exposure: Full sun to partial shade.
Soil: Sandy soil or clay loam; adaptable.
Soil Moisture: Moderate watering to dry.
Hardiness: USDA zones 4 to 8.
Elevation Range: Up to 7,000 feet.

Best Features

Symmetrical oval shape, glossy leaves, tolerates dry conditions very well, thornless. This species does not become weedy like the common buckthorn (*Rhamnus cathartica*).

Miscellaneous

Plants are typically grown from seeds; requires a sixty-day cold stratification for best germination.

Fruit attracts birds, and the tree provides shelter for birds.

Rhamnus smithii 47

Ribes uva-crispa L. 'Red Jacket'
COMANCHE gooseberry

As the edible berries grow they weigh the branches down, giving the plant an overall arching form.

Pronunciation: **RYE-bees oo-vah-CRISP-ah**

Family: **Saxifragaceae – saxifrage family**

Type of Plant: **Shrub**

Height: **2 to 3 feet**

Spread: **4 to 5 feet**

Published: *Species Plantarum* 1: 201. 1753. (for the species)

Year Recommended: **2001**

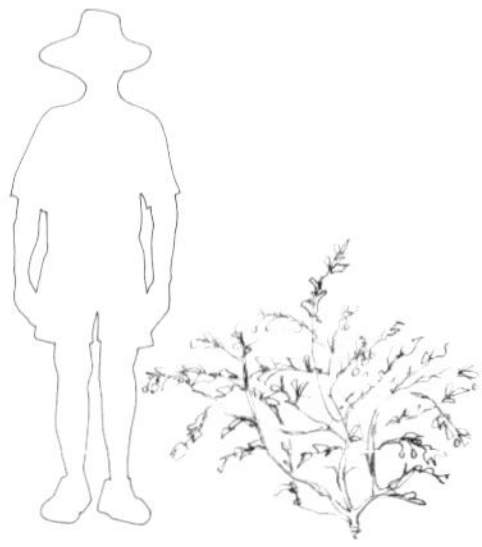

Why Chosen

The original Red Jacket gooseberry is a European cultivar that was selected in England prior to 1881. During the 1930s, a large collection of various gooseberry cultivars was assembled at the newly opened USDA Horticultural Field Station in Cheyenne, Wyoming, to evaluate, among other criteria, adaptability to regional climatic conditions. 'Red Jacket' proved to have superior hardiness. Its sweet, nickel-sized berries are produced in such abundance that the weight of the fruit causes the branches to become nearly prostrate. It is extremely thorny, bearing thick, heavy thorns in triplets at each node. This selection is also relatively resistant to powdery mildew.

Leaves and fruits as they appear in midsummer. Note the substantial thorns.

Landscape Use

Nice in an orchard or bramble patch, naturalistic landscape, as foundation or barrier plantings, or in wildlife plantings.

Form

Stout, erect to gently arching stems that become reclining with ascending tips when laden with fruit, forming a graceful mound.

Native Range of Species

Most parts of mountainous Europe, the Atlas Mountains of northern Africa, into temperate Asia; 5,900 to 8,200 feet.

Characteristics

Flowers: White to greenish pink, axillary clusters of one to three, early spring.
Leaves: Alternate, deeply three- to five-lobed, to 2 inches broad, usually covered with short, soft hairs, bright green, deciduous.
Stems: Erect to gently arching, armed with 2-inch stout and thick thorns in triplets at the nodes, bristly when young.
Fruits: Berries, oval, red, with prickles, ½ to 1 inch in diameter, midsummer; edible, very sweet.

Culture

Exposure: Full sun to partial shade.
Soil: Sandy or clay loams are best.
Soil Moisture: Moderate watering.
Hardiness: USDA zones 3 to 9.
Elevation Range: Up to 9,000 feet.

Best Features

Large, sweet fruits produced in abundance in midsummer.

Disadvantages

Extreme thorns; susceptible to aphids and spider mites.

Miscellaneous

These plants are typically grown from semi-hardwood cuttings taken in June. Plants can be grown from seeds but have a double dormancy and can be difficult to germinate.

Widely cultivated for its delicious fruits, which are used in desserts, for preserves, and for wine making.

This cultivar should not be confused with the four other clones or the cultivar of the same name that originated in Canada.

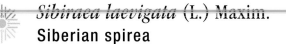

Sibiraea laevigata (L.) Maxim.
Siberian spirea

Upright stems bearing leathery leaves give this shrub a unique appearance.

Pronunciation: **sib-er-EE-ah LAY-vih-gah-tah**

Family: **Rosaceae – rose family**

Type of Plant: **Shrub**

Height: **4 to 5 feet**

Spread: **6 to 8 feet**

Published: ***Trudy Imperatorskago Saint-Peterburgskago Botaničeskago Sada*** **6(1): 215–216. 1879.**

Year Recommended: **2002**

Why Chosen

Siberian spirea is notable for its large, leathery, gray-green, lanceolate leaves. It produces panicles of showy greenish white flowers with a spicy fragrance from the current year's growth in early summer. The male flowers are somewhat larger than the female flowers. Small dry follicles follow after flowering. Of additional interest, especially in the winter, is the scaly, cracked, cinnamon-colored bark. This beautiful shrub was first acquired by the USDA Cheyenne Horticultural Field Station (now the High Plains Arboretum) in Wyoming many decades ago for observation. Gary Epstein and Scott Skogerboe (Fort Collins Wholesale Nursery) recognized the potential of this little-known plant and recommended it to Plant Select.

Landscape Use

Nice as an accent plant in middle to background of dry perennial border, rock gardens, or foundation plantings; best for informal settings.

Form

Naturally mounding, with architectural branching.

Native Range of Species

Endemic to the Altai Mountains of western Siberia, extending to eastern Kazakhstan and south to north-central China, with disjunct populations in western Yugoslavia; on calcareous cliffs, in open mountain valleys, and on mountain slopes; sometimes forming large thickets; 2,620 to 13,100 feet.

Left: The bluish gray-green leaf color is enhanced by late afternoon light.
Right: The flowers' spicy fragrance adds a note of complexity to the landscape.

Characteristics

Flowers: Showy greenish white flowers with yellow centers, to 1/5 inch across, in panicles to 3 inches long, fragrant, June.
Leaves: Alternate, oblong to lanceolate, to 3 inches long, entire, leathery, without hairs, bluish gray-green, deciduous.
Stems: Without hairs.
Bark: Scaly, cracked, cinnamon colored.
Fruits: Dry follicles to 1/5 inch long, July through late summer.

Culture

Exposure: Full sun to partial shade.
Soil: Sandy soil or clay loam; adaptable.
Soil Moisture: Moderate watering to dry.
Hardiness: USDA zones 4 to 8.
Elevation Range: Up to 7,000 feet.

Best Features

Beautiful leaf color and texture. Tolerates hot and dry situations. Coarse habit is a striking contrast to finely textured plants. Very cold tolerant.

Disadvantages

Does not perform well in dense, poorly drained soils.

Miscellaneous

Plants can be grown from seeds, but the germination process can be tedious and the seedlings are highly variable. Consistent plants are assured from stem cuttings, but they can be challenging to root.

The leaves are used by local populations in Asia as a substitute for tea.

Viburnum ×rhytidophylloides Suring. 'Alleghany'
Alleghany viburnum

Alleghany viburnum's year of beauty begins in midspring, with a profusion of white flowers borne in dense clusters.

Pronunciation: **vy-BUR-num rye-tid-oh-fil-LOY-deez**

Family: **Caprifoliaceae – honeysuckle family**

Type of Plant: **Herbaceous shrub**

Height: **8 to 10 feet**

Spread: **8 to 10 feet**

Published: *Jaarboek Nederlandische Dendrologische Vereeniging* **3: 140. 1927. (for the hybrid, not the cultivar)**

Year Recommended: **1997**

Why Chosen

Dr. Donald R. Egolf (US National Arboretum) selected 'Alleghany' from seedlings of *V. lantana* 'Mohican' × *V. rhytidophyllum* in 1958. It can produce hundreds of clustered, showy creamy-white flowers in May that are followed by deep red fruits by summer's end. The dark green leathery leaves often turn bronze or purple in the winter and persist most years well into spring, even in relatively sunny sites. Unlike most broadleaf evergreens, 'Alleghany' grows surprisingly well in sunny sites and on soils that have only been moderately amended with compost. It is not as sensitive to alkaline soils as other broadleaf evergreens.

Close examination of one cyme reveals the beauty of each flower.

Late summer brings on red fruit contrasting with the rich, leathery green leaves for a delight to the eyes.

In fall (left) the leaves turn purplish and will persist through the winter (right).

Landscape Use

Excellent as an informal screen or hedge, windbreak, the background of perennial and shrub borders, or as boundary or barrier plantings.

Form

Upright, densely branched; globose.

Native Range of Species

Of hybrid origin. The female parent, *V. lantana*, occurs from Europe to western Asia, and the male parent, *V. rhytidophyllum*, occurs in central and western China.

Characteristics

Flowers: Tubular, creamy white, in many-flowered 3- to 4-inch cymes held above the leaves, late May to early June.

Leaves: Opposite, broadly elliptic, entire, glossy above, with densely woolly brown hairs beneath, leathery, wrinkled, dark green becoming purplish in winter, deciduous to semi-persistent.

Stems: Erect, branched, covered densely with woolly hairs when young.

Fruits: Drupes, changing from green to brilliant red and ultimately to black, August through fall.

Culture

Exposure: Sun to shade.

Soil: Average garden soil.

Soil Moisture: Moist to average.

Hardiness: USDA zones 4b to 9.

Elevation Range: Up to 7,000 feet.

Best Features

Vigorous, essentially evergreen, dark green leathery and wrinkled leaves. Rapid growth rate. Hardy, dense growth habit. Tolerant of sunny and shady exposures. Flower buds for the following spring are prominent all through summer, fall, and winter.

Disadvantages

The flowers do not have a particularly pleasant fragrance.

Miscellaneous

This cultivar is propagated from semi-hardwood cuttings that do not have flower buds. Rooted cuttings should be held in a protected greenhouse for the first winter.

In dry climates, retain soil moisture with a 2-inch mulch of wood chips or leaves.

The *-oides* suffix on the species' name is from Greek and means "resembling." It makes reference to the leaves resembling those of *V. rhytidophyllum*, whose name is Greek for "with wrinkled leaves."

Viburnum ×rhytidophylloides 'Alleghany' 53

Xanthoceras sorbifolium Bunge 'Psgan'
Clear Creek golden yellowhorn

The luxurious flowers and lacy-textured leaves belie this tree's hardiness.

Pronunciation: **zan-THO-sir-as sor-bih-FOE-lee-um**

Family: **Sapindaceae – soapberry family**

Type of Plant: **Large shrub or small tree**

Height: **18 to 22 feet**

Spread: **10 to 15 feet**

Published: *Mémoires de l'Académie Imperiale des Sciences de Saint-Pétersbourg Divers Savans* 2: 85. 1835. (for the species)

Year Introduced: **2007**

Why Chosen

The plant is extremely eye-catching when the beautiful flowers appear in April and May. Nearly 1-inch-wide fragrant flowers are produced on 6- to 10-inch-long racemes in spring. Each has five bright white petals with a basal blotch that changes from yellow to red. The fruit is a three-valved, thick-walled 2- to 3-inch-diameter capsule containing several dark brown, large-pea-sized seeds in each cell. The featherlike leaves are a lustrous dark green color and provide a lacy-textured backdrop for the flowers and fruit. This especially hardy strain was selected at Green Acres Nursery, formerly in Golden, Colorado.

Left: The fragrant flowers are generally produced in abundance.

Right: Winter reveals a stout, irregularly branched tree holding its fruits throughout most of the winter.

The basal blotch of each flower changes from yellow to red.

Landscape Use

Ideal as a small specimen tree, the focal point in shrub planting, in small groupings in large lawns, or in the dappled shade at the edge of woodlands.

Form

Irregularly branched large shrub to small tree; globose.

Native Range of Species

North-central to northeastern China; mountain slopes; introduced to cultivation in 1866.

Characteristics

Flowers: Five-petaled, ¾ to 1 inch across, white with basal blotch that changes from yellow to red, borne in many-flowered raceme 6 to 10 inches long, fragrant, April to May.

Leaves: Alternate, pinnately compound, to about 1 foot long, lustrous green, persist late into fall, deciduous.

Stems: Branching pattern is stiff, irregular, and coarse.

Fruits: Capsules, globose, three-valved, 2 to 3 inches in diameter, dark brown seeds are slightly larger than peas, late summer to fall.

Culture

Exposure: Full sun to partial shade.

Soil: Garden loam, clay, or sandy soil.

Soil Moisture: Moderate watering to xeric.

Hardiness: USDA zones 5 to 8.

Elevation Range: Up to 6,000 feet.

Best Features

Striking large, blotched flowers. Foliage persists late into the fall. Branching habit is very architectural.

Disadvantages

Fruits are exceptionally attractive to squirrels.

Miscellaneous

Seed germination is enhanced by three months of moist, cold stratification. Grow seedlings in pots the first year, protect well the first winter, and transplant to a permanent location the following spring. Root cuttings are an alternative means of increase.

Flowers and leaves may be boiled for food; seeds have high nutritional value and can be roasted or boiled. They supposedly taste a little like chestnuts.

Sᴜɴsᴇᴛ hyssop.

Perennials

Clockwise from top left:
Prairie Jewel penstemon,
silver sage, Coronado hyssop,
Spanish Peaks foxglove,
Prairie Jewel penstemon.

Agastache aurantiaca (A. Gray) Linton & Epling
Coronado hyssop

Golden yellow and orange trumpet-shaped flowers on airy stems will begin to grace the garden in late summer and continue until frost.

Pronunciation: **ah-GAS-tah-key or-an-tee-AH-cah**

Family: **Lamiaceae – mint family**

Type of Plant: **Herbaceous perennial**

Height: **15 to 18 inches**

Spread: **12 to 15 inches**

Published: ***American Midland Naturalist*** **33: 225. 1945.**

Year Introduced: **2001**

Why Chosen

Seeds of this species were purchased by Denver Botanic Gardens in 1991 from Sallie Walker's seed list; she is a seed collector from Tucson, Arizona. Although *Agastache aurantiaca* is native in northern Mexico, it seems to possess greater hardiness than its natural range would indicate. The wonderful blend of yellow and orange in the flowers justifies growing it, even as an annual. It grows into a shimmering mound of yellow and orange trumpets in late summer. The foliage is intensely aromatic when brushed against.

Landscape Use

Suitable as a foundation plant, in wildlife plantings, in massings, or in the middle of a perennial border.

Form

Spreading, open, airy upright stems form a rounded or vaselike shape.

Native Range of Species

Sierra Madre Occidental of southwestern Chihuahua and western Durango, Mexico; common in rocky fields, on plateaus, and on canyon summits in open pine-oak woodlands; 6,550 to 8,200 feet.

Characteristics

Flowers: Tubular, golden yellow and orange, to 1 inch long, summer to fall.
Leaves: Opposite, triangular-ovate, 1 to 1½ inches long, covered sparsely with downy gray hairs above and moderately below, aromatic.
Stems: Woody at the base, producing thin but sturdy herbaceous shoots perennially.
Fruits: Four nutlets.

Culture

Exposure: Full sun to partial shade.
Soil: Average garden soil.
Soil Moisture: Moderate watering to dry.
Hardiness: USDA zones 4b to 8.
Elevation Range: Up to 7,000 feet.

Best Features

Long season of color. Attractive form and habit. Drought tolerant.

Disadvantages

Sensitive to excess moisture. Not reliably hardy in colder areas. Can be short-lived.

Miscellaneous

Plants grown from seeds by most nurseries are from a stable seed source. Seeds will germinate best without cover. Cuttings are also a viable option. Very attractive to butterflies.

The flowers' color is outstanding against the green and blue leaves of the garden.

Agastache aurantiaca 59

Agastache cana (Hook.) Wooton & Standl. 'Sinning'[PP13,673]
SONORAN SUNSET hyssop

SONORAN SUNSET hyssop is more compact, blooms longer, and has larger flowers than is typical of the species.

Pronunciation: **ah-GAS-tah-key CAN-ah**

Family: **Lamiaceae – mint family**

Type of Plant: **Herbaceous perennial**

Height: **15 to 18 inches**

Spread: **12 to 15 inches**

Published: ***Contributions from the United States National Herbarium* 16: 166. 1913. (for the species)**

Year Introduced: **2002**

Why Chosen

Known commonly as Double Bubble mint for its aromatic foliage and flowers, *Agastache cana* has become a popular plant in recent years. This species is quite variable and has often hybridized with other species in the genus. From a large planting of pure *A. cana* at Welby Gardens (Denver, Colorado), Duane Sinning, an employee at Welby at the time, selected an individual with much larger flowers, more compact habit of growth, and longer flowering season. This novel selection was subsequently shared with Plant Select. The vivid hot-magenta flowers of Sonoran Sunset hyssop appear in August and September, providing a stunning spectacle for borders and xeriscapes.

Purple iceplant (foreground) and Sunset hyssop (right) are an eye-catching combination with Sonoran Sunset hyssop (background).

Landscape Use

Excellent for massing, an attractive perennial for foundation plantings, as a middle border plant, in xeriscapes, or wildlife plantings.

Form

Spreading, open, airy upright stems form a rounded or vaselike shape.

Native Range of Species

Extreme western Texas and south-central New Mexico; in crevices, at the base of granite cliffs, or in protected box canyons; as part of the ecotone of upper desert scrub and lower oak-piñon zones; 4,600 to 6,500 feet.

Characteristics

Flowers: Tubular, to 1 inch long, lavender-rose, late summer to fall.
Leaves: Opposite, lanceolate to deltoid-ovate, to 1 inch long, covered sparsely with downy gray hairs above and moderately below, aromatic.
Stems: Woody at the base, producing an abundance of thin herbaceous shoots perennially.
Fruits: Four nutlets.

Culture

Exposure: Full sun to partial shade.
Soil: Average garden soil (ordinary or sandy loam or dry clay).
Soil Moisture: Moderate watering to dry.
Hardiness: USDA zones 5 to 9.
Elevation Range: Up to 6,000 feet.

Best Features

Long bloom period. Bruised foliage gives off a rich Dubble Bubble Gum fragrance.

Disadvantages

Intolerant of wet conditions.

Miscellaneous

This patented selection must be propagated from cuttings to maintain genetic purity. Cuttings can rot easily if kept too wet.

Very attractive to hummingbirds, butterflies, hawk moths, and other insects, especially bees.

Agastache rupestris (Greene) Standl.
Sunset hyssop

The flowers of Sunset hyssop are delightful.

Pronunciation: **ah-GAS-tah-key rue-PES-tris**

Family: **Lamiaceae – mint family**

Type of Plant: **Herbaceous perennial**

Height: **20 to 24 inches**

Spread: **8 to 15 inches**

Published: ***Contributions from the United States National Herbarium** 13: 212. 1910. (for the species)*

Year Recommended: **1997**

Why Chosen

"Instant classic" is perhaps the best way to describe this unusual western wildflower. First collected by Sallie Walker, a Tuscon, Arizona, seed collector, the seeds were shared with Plant Select in 1993. The first year's planting in the Rock Alpine Garden at Denver Botanic Gardens was so spectacular and produced such a bumper crop of seeds that it helped launch the 1997 inaugural year of Plant Select offerings, featured on the front of the brochure, no less! The flamelike clusters of flowers, reminiscent of Indian paintbrush, consist of long-tubed corollas colored a rusty orange with hints of yellow, red, and lavender—a stunning combination.

Sunset hyssop (left) adds colorful balance to this lovely dry garden.

Landscape Use

Excellent intermediate-height perennial for the middle to background of perennial borders. Good for dry, sunny locations.

Form

Spreading, open, airy upright stems form a rounded or vaselike shape.

Native Range of Species

Mountains of southern Arizona, southwestern New Mexico, and possibly northeastern Sonora, Mexico; in sandy soil at the base of protected north-facing slopes in upper oak-savanna, piñon-juniper, or lower ponderosa pine zones; 4,900 to 6,550 feet.

Characteristics

Flowers: Tubular, sunset orange and mauve, to about 1 inch long, late July to frost.
Leaves: Opposite, narrowly lanceolate to linear, 1 to 2 inches long, covered sparsely with downy gray hairs above and moderately below, aromatic.
Stems: Woody at the base, producing an abundance of herbaceous shoots perennially.
Fruits: Four nutlets.

Culture

Exposure: Full sun to partial shade (preferring at least a half-day's sun).
Soil: Average garden soil (ordinary to poor soil); well-drained soils.
Soil Moisture: Moderate watering to dry.
Hardiness: USDA zones 4b to 10.
Elevation Range: Up to 7,000 feet.

Best Features

Widely adaptable to various soils and sun exposures. Extremely drought and heat tolerant. Long season of bloom.

Disadvantages

Intolerant of wet conditions.

Miscellaneous

Plants are grown from seeds, requiring light to germinate, or from stem tip cuttings, which yield more-uniform plants.

Leaves smell like licorice.

Aquilegia chrysantha A. Gray
DENVER GOLD columbine

DENVER GOLD columbine is a good choice among columbines because it tolerates a wide variety of growing conditions.

Pronunciation: **a-queh-LEE-jah chris-AN-thah**

Family: **Ranunculaceae – buttercup family**

Type of Plant: **Herbaceous perennial**

Height: **30 to 36 inches**

Spread: **15 to 20 inches**

Published: *Proceedings of the American Academy of Arts and Sciences* 8: 621. 1873. (for the species)

Year Recommended: **2001**

Why Chosen

Most gardeners cherish the Colorado state flower (*Aquilegia caerulea*), although plantings of this species quickly hybridize. Over the years, extensive plantings of this "other" showy Rocky Mountain columbine at Denver Botanic Gardens have not only remained stable, but have exceeded expectations. Denver Gold columbine has a much longer blooming season and thrives in a wide range of conditions. The luminous yellow flowers are similar in shape and size to *A. caerulea*, although the plants can be larger, lusher, and very long-lived. This species has consistently proven to be the most resilient columbine for landscape use.

Left: Flowers are long lasting and even have a second showing, particularly if the first flush is deadheaded.

Right: Partial shade is ideal for Denver Gold columbine and companion plant coral bells.

Landscape Use

Best used in mass plantings in dappled shade.

Form

Robust, mounding perennial.

Native Range of Species

Colorado, Utah, Arizona, New Mexico, Texas, and northwestern Mexico; in damp places in canyons, especially along streams or in rocky ravines; 3,275 to 11,460 feet.

Characteristics

Flowers: Sepals and petals golden yellow, 1½ to 2¾ inches across, sepals with long spurs, May to June, with heavy rebloom later.
Leaves: Alternate, mostly triternately compound, blue-green, basal 3½ to 18 inches long.
Stems: Rigid, erect, 30 to 36 inches tall, pale green, often covered with a bloom that can be rubbed off.
Fruits: Follicles to about 1 inch long, beaks to ½ inch long.

Culture

Exposure: Full sun to deep shade.
Soil: Sandy soil or clay loam (not fussy).
Soil Moisture: Moderate watering.
Hardiness: USDA zones 3 to 8.
Elevation Range: Up to 9,000 feet.

Best Features

Long season of bloom. Very adaptable to various soils and conditions. Much more stable in flower color and habit than other columbines and less likely to hybridize.

Disadvantages

Seedlings can come up thickly in ideal situations and are best planted in masses, since they can smother smaller plants. Susceptible to aphid infestations.

Miscellaneous

Columbine seeds tend to have very complex dormancies. This one, however, is relatively easy to germinate. Using the freshest seeds possible, give a two-week cold, moist stratification before sowing.

Capable of producing cyanide (cyanogenetic).

Aquilegia chrysantha 65

Aquilegia L. 'Swan Violet & White'
REMEMBRANCE columbine

Although REMEMBRANCE columbine's blooming season is short, the sheer beauty of its flowers make it a worthy landscape plant.

Pronunciation: **a-queh-LEE-jah**

Family: **Ranunculaceae – buttercup family**

Type of Plant: **Herbaceous perennial**

Height: **14 to 24 inches**

Spread: **15 to 18 inches**

Year Introduced: **2001**

R. L. Sanford

Why Chosen

REMEMBRANCE columbine was named in memory of the victims of the Columbine High School tragedy in 1999 (Littleton, Colorado). The parents of this selection both came from the Songbirds columbine series, produced by Ball Horticultural Company. Charlie Weddle developed the female parent (also used for 'Blue Jay') in which *Aquilegia caerulea* figured prominently. The male parent was developed by Ellen Leue, who crossed 'Blue Bird' (predominantly *A. caerulea*) with 'Pretty Bird' (*A. caerulea* and nearly pure *A. canadensis*) and inbred the line to get a fairly dark blue recombination. The resulting hybrid has strong violet-purple sepals and spurs clasping the pure white petals and golden boss of stamens.

Left: Violet-purple, white, and yellow are an unmatched combination in columbines.

Right: REMEMBRANCE columbine's handsome form will last only a short time after flowers fade. Cut foliage back as it withers to make room for annuals or later perennials.

Landscape Use

Nice as a border perennial for shade or partially shaded areas.

Form

Robust mounding perennial.

Native Range of Species

This cultivar is of hybrid origin. The parents' nativities are *Aquilegia caerulea*, Rocky Mountains, and *A. canadensis*, Nova Scotia to Florida, west to Minnesota and Tennessee.

Characteristics

Flowers: White petals, rich, shining violet-purple sepals with long spurs, late spring to early summer.
Leaves: Alternate, mostly triternately compound, blue-green.
Stems: Rigid, erect, 14 to 24 inches tall, pale green, often covered with a bloom that can be rubbed off.
Fruits: Follicles, to about 1 inch long, beaked.

Culture

Exposure: Partial sun.
Soil: Loamy, well-drained soils are best.
Soil Moisture: Moderate watering.
Hardiness: USDA zones 3 to 9.
Elevation Range: Up to 9,000 feet.

Best Features

Striking deep violet-blue and pure white flowers are atypical for the genus. The delicate meadow rue–like foliage is decorative all summer.

Disadvantages

Not long-lived, and will not come consistently true from seeds produced in the garden. Susceptible to aphid infestations and powdery mildew. Flowering season is relatively short.

Miscellaneous

Most commercially available seeds of this columbine are already primed and will germinate readily. It is possible to divide columbines, but it is usually very difficult to separate the crowded crowns and maintain enough roots to support growth.

Previously listed as 'Colorado Violet & White' by Plant Select.

Aquilegia 'Swan Violet & White' 67

Berlandiera lyrata Benth.
Chocolate flower

Pronunciation: **ber-land-ee-AIR-ah lye-RAH-tah**

Family: **Asteraceae – sunflower family**

Type of Plant: **Herbaceous perennial**

Height: **10 to 20 inches**

Spread: **10 to 20 inches**

Published: *Plantas Hartwegianas Imprimis Mexicanas* **17. 1839.**

Year Recommended: **2004**

Why Chosen

Chocolate flower is a must-have plant for chocoholics everywhere. The tantalizing floral aroma of chocolate is most intense during the morning hours. The daisylike, pale yellow heads with dark eyes are produced continuously from early June to late autumn and make this an irresistible selection. After pollination, the flowers transform into rounded chartreuse seed heads that add textural interest to the floral display. The trim rosettes of sage green to silvery gray leaves are attractive, even when the plant is not in bloom. Drought and heat tolerance and the plant's ability to naturalize further enhance its value in the garden.

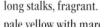

Flowers will emit a distinctive chocolate aroma, particularly during the morning hours.

Landscape Use

Best planted in groups or drifts, in the foreground, close to foot traffic along walkway edges, and in raised planters to maximize its sensory appeal. An ideal plant for meadow or prairie plantings. Perfect for "hell strips."

Form

Compact, low-mounding rosette.

Native Range of Species

Kansas, Oklahoma, Texas, Colorado, New Mexico, Arizona, south into Mexico; in dry, sandy loams, rocky limestone soils; roadsides, grasslands with mesquite, oak, and juniper; 2,300 to 7,200 feet.

Characteristics

Flowers: Daisylike heads, solitary on long stalks, fragrant. Ray flowers are pale yellow with maroon stripes on veins beneath. Disk flowers are red to maroon, creating the "eye." The heads nod and become erect after the ray flowers fade, changing to chartreuse when in seed, May to September.
Leaves: Alternate, oblanceolate or obovate to spatulate, often lyrate, covered thinly with woolly gray hairs beneath, forming compact rosettes, soft sage green to silvery gray.
Stems: Slender green stems, erect, sprawling, or prostrate with ascending tips.
Fruits: Obovate achenes.

Culture

Exposure: Full sun to partial shade.
Soil: Poor, dry soil.
Soil Moisture: Prefers dry conditions (minimal or no water).
Hardiness: USDA zones 4 to 9.
Elevation Range: Up to 7,000 feet.

Best Features

The chocolate fragrance is most intense during the morning hours. Long cycle of blooming through the summer. Thrives in hot and dry situations.

Disadvantages

Can be exceptionally attractive to bees. These plants need to be grown without fertilizer or water once established or they will get leggy.

Miscellaneous

This is a seed-grown native plant. Seeds will germinate quickly and readily at almost any time of the year. Keep seeds covered during the germinating process.

Used by Native Americans for stomach ailments. Smoke from dried, burned roots used to calm nervousness and stimulate courage. The flowers are combined with sausage as a seasoning.

Dianthus L. 'First Love'
First Love dianthus

First Love dianthus is an easy-to-grow perennial.

Pronunciation: **di-ANN-thus**

Family: **Caryophyllaceae – pink family**

Type of Plant: **Herbaceous perennial**

Height: **15 to 20 inches**

Spread: **15 to 18 inches**

Year Recommended: **2001**

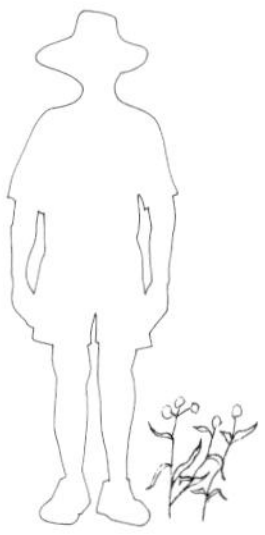

Why Chosen

First Love dianthus (*Dianthus barbatus* × *D. superbus*) was developed by Akio Ito, a renowned plant breeder of Takii Seed Co. Ltd. It has three distinctive characteristics that distinguish it from other dianthus: unique, reverse flower coloring (changing from white to soft pink, then gradually to rosy pink), a long flowering season, and excellent performance as a cut flower. 'First Love' is Ito's tribute to a young girl he remembered who blushed while speaking of her first love; the flowers mirror her complexion. It was introduced in the company's Japanese flower catalog in 1990 and in the worldwide catalog in 2005.

Flowering begins in early spring and, with regular deadheading, will give season-long color to the garden. It is wonderful as a drift through the garden or as a border along a path, where its fragrance can be appreciated.

Landscape Use

Attractive as a mass planting, in drifts, planters, or raised beds; site close to paths, where the exquisite fragrance can be appreciated.

Form

Low-mounding perennial with many basal stems. Each is wiry but very strong and wind resistant.

Native Range of Species

This cultivar is of hybrid origin. The parents' nativities are *Dianthus barbatus*, Pyrenees, Carpathian Mountains, Balkan Peninsula, and *D. superbus,* Italy and Romania, north to Scandinavia, east to Russia and Japan.

Characteristics

Flowers: Soft, lacy-edged petals make up flowers about 1 inch in diameter, borne in clusters, petals change from white to soft pink and gradually to rosy pink, fragrant, April through frost.

Leaves: Opposite, often united at base into a sheath, congested at crown, narrow, dark green, continuing up the stem, basal leaves persist through the winter.

Stems: Thin and wiry, but strong and wind resistant.

Fruits: Four-valved cylindrical capsules.

Culture

Exposure: Sun to partial shade.
Soil: Ordinary garden loam.
Soil Moisture: Moderate watering.
Hardiness: USDA zones 3b to 9.
Elevation Range: Up to 10,000 feet.

Best Features

Although best grown as an annual, clumps can persist for two, three, or more years, albeit with diminishing returns. Judicious deadheading will ensure a long blooming season. Flowers change color in reverse order to typical dianthus, making this cultivar a novelty. Can be used as cut flowers.

Disadvantages

Short-lived perennial.

Miscellaneous

Must be grown from commercially available seeds or from cuttings to maintain genetic integrity.

Diascia integerrima Benth.

CORAL CANYON twinspur

Pronunciation: **die-ASS-key-ah in-teh-ger-REE-mah**

Family: **Scrophulariaceae – figwort family**

Type of Plant: **Herbaceous perennial**

Height: **12 to 18 inches**

Spread: **10 to 12 inches**

Published: *Companion to the Botanical Magazine. ii.* **18. 1836.**
           (for the species, not the compact form)

Year Introduced: **2000**

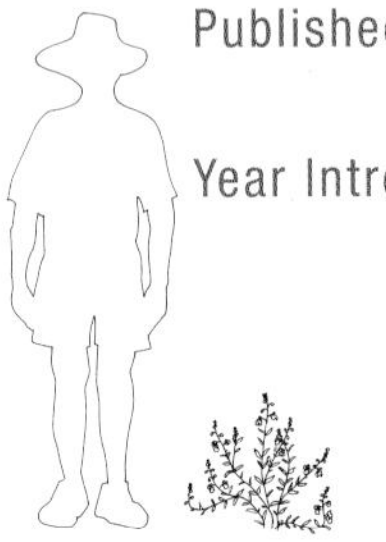

Why Chosen

In March of 1996, Panayoti Kelaidis (Denver Botanic Gardens) encountered a much smaller form of the yard-tall species on a high ridge of the Drakensberg Mountains, not far from Rhodes, in the East Cape province of South Africa. The collected strain proved to be less than half as tall as the typical form. An especially trim clone was subsequently selected for Plant Select and given the trademark name CORAL CANYON. The masses of delicate, coral-colored blossoms are produced with the vigor of an annual from May to frost, with a bit of deadheading. *Twinspur* refers to the paired floral spurs, and the species' name means "absolutely entire," describing the perfectly smooth leaf margins. David Salman (president, High Country Gardens and Santa Fe Greenhouses in Santa Fe, New Mexico) proclaims this plant to be the best introduction from South Africa.

CORAL CANYON twinspur and COLORADO GOLD gazania make a great long-lasting combination in sunny gardens.

Culture

Exposure: Full sun to partial shade.
Soil: Garden loam.
Soil Moisture: Moderate watering.
Hardiness: USDA zones 4b to 8.
Elevation Range: Up to 7,000 feet.

Best Features

Long flowering season. Properly sited it can persist for five or more years in the same spot. Remarkable hardiness compared with other commercially available varieties. Tolerates a wide range of soil moisture.

Disadvantages

Short-lived perennial. Benefits from judicious pruning in mid- to late summer.

Miscellaneous

Plants can be grown from either seeds or cuttings. If grown with other diascia selections, propagate from cuttings, as the different plants will likely hybridize.

    Diascia is a relative newcomer to North American gardens. Along with *Delosperma* and *Agastache*, essentially unknown in the United States in the 1970s, they are now found in many gardens.

Landscape Use

Excellent for mass plantings and drifts, in the foreground to middle of perennial borders, rock gardens, and planters.

Form

Many-branched, low-mounding perennial.

Native Range of Species

Natal, Cape, Lesotho, Transvaal, and Orange Free State provinces of South Africa; on cliffs, rocky areas, near small streams; 4,000 to 7,000 feet.

Characteristics

Flowers: Oval, twin-spurred, about ⅓ inch long, soft pink with a deep pink throat, in terminal racemes, from May to frost.
Leaves: Opposite, lanceolate to ovate-oblong, entire, with perfectly smooth margins, ½ to ¾ inch long.
Stems: Ascending, rigid, erect.
Fruits: Ovoid-oblong, dry capsules to ⅖ inch long.

Digitalis obscura L.
SUNSET foxglove

A rich blend of floral color gives SUNSET foxglove its name.

Pronunciation: **dij-eh-TAL-iss ob-SCUR-ah**

Family: **Scrophulariaceae – figwort family**

Type of Plant: **Herbaceous perennial**

Height: **14 to 24 inches**

Spread: **15 to 20 inches**

Published: ***Species Plantarum*, ed. 2: 867. 1763.**

Year Recommended: **2004**

Why Chosen

The great British collectors Jim and Jenny Archibald introduced this species in the early 1980s from a collection they made in Andalucia, Spain. Seeds from their collection quickly produced vigorous clumps at Denver Botanic Gardens, performing particularly well in sunny and even xeric sites. The plant's habit is somewhat shrubby, with substantial, almost waxy dark green willowy leaves. The amazing trumpet-shaped flowers are burnt sienna suffused with bright gold and reddish highlights. It flowers profusely from late June to August, with scattered blooms appearing up to first frost.

Left: Wiry stems support a cascade of bell-shaped flowers throughout the summer.

Right: Clumps of SUNSET foxglove provide a strong focal point in the garden.

Landscape Use

Nice as a border perennial; also good in rock gardens.

Form

Nearly shrubby producing basal rosettes of foliage with branching, upright flower stems.

Native Range of Species

Central, eastern, and southern Spain to northern Morocco; on limestone in high mountains; rare.

Characteristics

Flowers: Trumpet shaped, burnt sienna suffused with bright gold and reddish highlights, about 1 inch long, profuse from late June to August and scattered until first frost.
Leaves: Alternate, linear-lanceolate, 4 to 5 inches long, in rosettes, leathery, evergreen.
Stems: Wiry and branched, with a smooth, leathery texture.
Fruits: Capsules to about ⅔ inch long.

Culture

Exposure: Full sun to partial shade.
Soil: Garden loam, clay, or sandy soil; well drained.
Soil Moisture: Moderate watering to dry.
Hardiness: USDA zones 4b to 9.
Elevation Range: Up to 7,000 feet.

Best Features

Few plants have such distinctively colored flowers; an example is the penstemons, which SUNSET foxglove closely resembles. The evergreen foliage provides yearlong interest. Very tolerant of drought and alkaline soils. Responds well to judicious shearing in spring before new growth begins.

Disadvantages

The foliage can sunburn if grown in extremely exposed sites.

Miscellaneous

Although plants can be produced from stem cuttings, this strain is a stable compact form that can be grown from seeds.

Useful as a cardiotonic.

Digitalis thapsi L.
SPANISH PEAKS foxglove

Small clusters of SPANISH PEAKS foxglove flowers are held gracefully over the open and airy plant structure.

Pronunciation: **dij-eh-TAL-iss THAP-see**

Family: **Scrophulariaceae – figwort family**

Type of Plant: **Herbaceous perennial**

Height: **12 to 15 inches**

Spread: **12 to 15 inches**

Published: *Species Plantarum*, ed. 2: 867. 1763

Year Introduced: **1999**

Why Chosen

Collected by Jim and Jenny Archibald in southern Iberia, this gorgeous foxglove tolerates a bit more sun than its well-known cousin, *Digitalis purpurea*. In contrast, it grows particularly well in that famous and challenging condition called dry shade. Like *D. obscura*, the blossoms on this Spanish foxglove have a gentle curve, like the stem of an old-fashioned smoking pipe. The typical flower color ranges from pale pink to deep rose in the wild, whereas this strain bears flowers that are a distinctive shade of raspberry, contrasting wonderfully with the viscid mats of golden-haired foliage.

Left: Spiked veronica, roses, and Shasta daisies grouped with Spanish Peaks foxglove make a lovely garden bouquet.

Right: The flowers are characteristically held on one side of the flower stem.

Landscape Use

Lovely as individuals for accent, massed, or in drifts, in rock gardens or among boulders.

Form

Spreading, open, airy upright flower stems form a rounded or vaselike shape.

Native Range of Species

South central Spain west to eastern Portugal; in acidic soil in natural areas.

Characteristics

Flowers: Tubular, 1 to 2 inches long, drooping along one-sided racemes, raspberry-colored, April to August.
Leaves: Alternate, broadly lanceolate, about 10 inches long and up to 1¾ inches wide, covered with yellow glandular hairs, produced in basal rosettes.
Stems: Upright, simple to branched, bearing leaves much smaller than in the basal rosette.
Fruits: Capsule to about ½ inch long.

Culture

Exposure: Sun to partial shade.
Soil: Ordinary garden loam.
Soil Moisture: Moderate watering.
Hardiness: USDA zones 4b to 9.
Elevation Range: Up to 7,000 feet.

Best Features

Performs exceptionally well in dry shade.

Miscellaneous

Foxglove seeds germinate best when exposed in good light environments. Seeds that are covered may fall victim to fungal pathogens.

Epilobium fleischeri Hochst.
Alpine willowherb

Alpine willowherb's flowers build slowly
to a crescendo from mid- to late July.

Pronunciation: **ep-ee-LOBE-ee-um FLYSH-er-eye**

Family: **Onagraceae – evening primrose family**

Type of Plant: **Herbaceous perennial**

Height: **18 to 20 inches**

Spread: **10 to 12 inches**

Published: *Flora Regensburgischen* 9: 25. 1826.

Year Recommended: **2002**

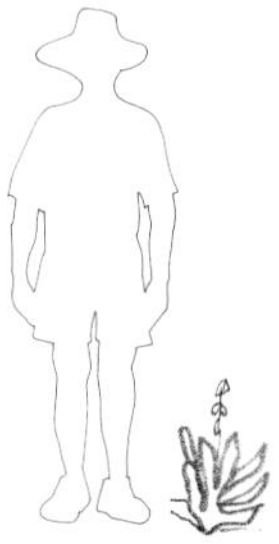

Why Chosen

Although alpine willowherb has been grown in European gardens for hundreds of years, it was virtually unknown in the United States. Denver Botanic Gardens acquired its seeds from Alpengarten Zenz (Graz-Grambach, Switzerland) in the 1980s. This diminutive, compact cousin of fireweed (*Epilobium angustifolium*) does not have its giant relative's weedy tendencies and is a true perennial. Finely textured gray-green foliage and wiry reddish stems provide the framework for delicate fuchsia-pink flowers that appear continuously from late spring into the fall. After the dry fruits dehisce, the "fluffy" seeds are carried away on the wind, providing yet another attractive trait that adds further interest as winter approaches.

Plants reach their full floral glory in midsummer, then bloom sporadically into fall, transforming into fluffy seed heads.

Landscape Use

Excellent for massing and drifts in the foreground or middle of the perennial border, among rocks, rock gardens, and in containers.

Form

Sprawling to low-mounding perennial.

Native Range of Species

Endemic to the Alps of central Europe, where it is fairly common; in gravels, moraines, and along watersides; common on acidic soils; 2,295 to 8,860 feet.

Characteristics

Flowers: Four-petaled, each petal obovate or elliptic, alternating with the sepals, delicate fuchsia-pink with red veins and prominent stamens, to 1 inch across, late spring to fall.
Leaves: Alternate, elliptic, finely toothed, gray-green.
Stems: Erect, rigid, distinctively reddish.
Fruits: Elongate capsules, seeds papillose.
Roots: Thick, prostrate rhizome.

Culture

Exposure: Full sun to partial shade.
Soil: Loamy or sandy soils are best.
Soil Moisture: Moderate watering.
Hardiness: USDA zones 3 to 8.
Elevation Range: Up to 8,000 feet.

Best Features

Alpine willowherb thrives in a wide range of soils, exposures, and habitats, from nearly alpine to xeric. It is compact and noninvasive, and surprisingly drought tolerant.

Disadvantages

Susceptible to flea beetles. May reseed locally.

Miscellaneous

Seeds are very easy to germinate. Once germinated, overwatering is the most common cause of attrition; seedlings need to dry thoroughly between waterings.

Pronunciation: **PEN-steh-mon grand-ih-FLOR-us**

Family: **Scrophulariaceae – figwort family**

Type of Plant: **Herbaceous perennial**

Height: **20 to 36 inches**

Spread: **8 to 12 inches**

Published: *Catalogue of Plants of Upper Louisiana* no. 64.
1813. (for the species, not this strain)

Year Introduced: **2000**

Why Chosen

There are few native penstemons that can rival PRAIRIE JEWEL penstemon in flower size and color, which ranges from white to deep violet-purple. The name honors Claude Barr, who authored the landmark publication *Jewels of the Plains*, and his favorite plant, *Penstemon grandiflorus*. Barr collected seeds of this species from the southern Black Hills of South Dakota and shared them with Mary Ann Heacock, an avid Denver gardener, in the early 1960s. This strain, the result of nearly thirty years of backyard breeding by Heacock, incorporates genes from the Seeba strain, *P. grandiflorus*, *P. kunthii*, *P. parryi*, and *P. murrayanus*, with repeated backcrossing to *P. grandiflorus*. It was brought to Plant Select by Kelly Grummons (Timberline Gardens, Arvada, Colorado). The species' name, *grandiflorus*, is Latin, meaning "large-flowered."

Left: Plants will remain stalwart and upright in sunny, somewhat dry locations.

Right: Brown, mature seed capsules complement the bluish green foliage.

Landscape Use

Suitable for mass planting or drifts, in the middle to back of a perennial border, or in midgrass meadows.

Form

Strongly upright, vertical, unbranched spire.

Native Range of Species

Illinois to North Dakota and Wyoming, south to Texas; in dry, sandy shortgrass and tallgrass habitats.

Characteristics

Flowers: Tubular with inflated throat, to 2 inches long, pure white through lavender, rose-pink, or a deep violet-purple, May and June.
Leaves: Opposite, basal obovate to 6 inches long, stem leaves broadly ovate to cordate clasping to 1½ inches broad, entire, without hairs, covered with a bloom that can be rubbed off, bluish green.
Stems: Sturdy, without hairs, somewhat covered with a bloom that can be rubbed off, bluish green.
Fruits: Capsules.

Culture

Exposure: Full sun.
Soil: Ordinary or sandy loam or dry clay.
Soil Moisture: Moderate watering to dry.
Hardiness: USDA zones 3 to 9.
Elevation Range: Up to 8,000 feet.

Best Features

Tolerates low water situations. Large flowers in an eye-catching range of colors.

Disadvantages

Does not tolerate wet soils; excessive watering encourages weak growth that is not self-supporting.

Miscellaneous

Plants are easily grown from seeds after pretreating with a thirty-day cold stratification or soaking for four hours in 500 ppm gibberellic acid.

Penstemon rostriflorus Kellogg
Bridges' penstemon

Late in the growing season, Bridges' penstemon makes its presence known with a swarm of orange-red flowers.

Pronunciation: **PEN-steh-mon ross-treh-FLOOR-us**

Family: **Scrophulariaceae – figwort family**

Type of Plant: **Herbaceous perennial**

Height: **24 to 36 inches**

Spread: **24 to 36 inches**

Published: *Hutching's California Magazine* 5(3): 102. 1860.

Year Recommended: **2006**

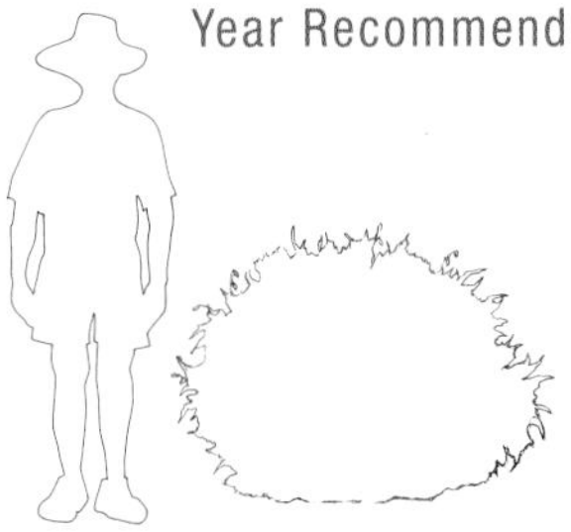

Sheila Payne

Why Chosen

Of the three red-flowered penstemons native to the southwestern United States, *Penstemon barbatus, P. eatonii* and *P. rostriflorus,* Bridges' penstemon may live the longest and also have the longest flowering season, lasting from late July through October. It forms an attractive, somewhat shrubby mound of 2- to 3-foot stems with linear green foliage. The 1-inch, strongly two-lipped, orange-red to scarlet flowers are produced in few to many false whorls (verticillasters) along the flowering stem. This penstemon tolerates a wide range of soil types and sites, is drought adapted, and performs best with at least a half day of sun. The eye-catching flowers are superb magnets for hummingbirds.

Landscape Use

Well suited to drifts and massing, short- to intermediate-grass meadows, native landscapes, xeric plantings, and as the background of a dry perennial border.

Form

Attractive, somewhat shrubby mound.

Bridges' penstemon's showy flowers are a beautiful contrast to white (allium) and yellow (goldenrod).

Culture

Exposure: Full sun to partial shade.
Soil: Garden loam, clay, or sandy soil.
Soil Moisture: Moderate watering to very dry.
Hardiness: USDA zones 4b to 8.
Elevation Range: Up to 7,000 feet.

Best Features

Very long-lived. Long flowering season that continues later than most penstemons.

Miscellaneous

Plants can be grown from seeds or cuttings; seeds must receive a thirty-day cold stratification to break the physiological dormancy before sowing.

Native Americans used a preparation from the roots to treat swollen limbs.

Magnet for hummingbirds.

Native Range of Species

Southwest Colorado, northwest New Mexico, northern Arizona, eastern California, southern Nevada, and southern Utah; in a diverse range of dryland plant communities; 3,275 to 10,300 feet.

Characteristics

Flowers: Tubular, two-lipped, to 1¼ inches long, upper lobes appearing beaklike, orange-red to scarlet, midsummer to fall.
Leaves: Opposite, oblanceolate to spatulate, entire, mostly without hairs, to 3½ inches long.
Stems: Erect to ascending from woody base, mostly without hairs.
Fruits: Capsule.

Penstemon ×mexicali

PIKES PEAK PURPLE penstemon

Late afternoon sunlight highlights the already bright violet-purple flowers of this hybrid.

Pronunciation: **PEN-steh-mon MEX-ih-cal-ee**

Family: **Scrophulariaceae – figwort family**

Type of Plant: **Herbaceous perennial**

Height: **12 to 18 inches**

Spread: **10 to 15 inches**

Year Introduced: **1999**

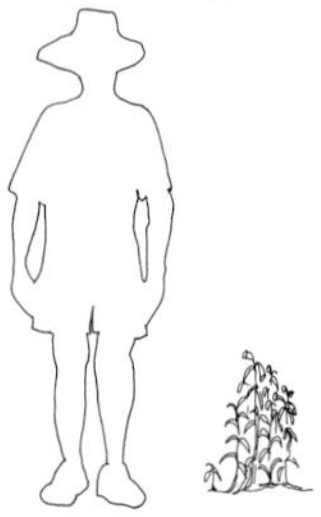

Why Chosen

Bruce Meyers (White Salmon, Washington) was an amateur hybridizer who spent many years hybridizing various extremely showy Mexican penstemons, which lack hardiness, with very hardy American species. The "Mexicali" hybrids are the result of these crosses, combining the large flowers of the Mexican parents with the vigor and hardiness of the northern parents. Their hybrid vigor has resulted in plants that grow and bloom continuously throughout the summer. They tolerate much more water than most wild penstemons, although they can easily endure drought as well. PIKES PEAK PURPLE penstemon was selected from a RED ROCKS penstemon population at Welby Gardens (Denver, Colorado) for its bright violet-purple flowers.

Left: PIKES PEAK PURPLE penstemon is quite handsome in combination with blue oat grass.

Landscape Use

Ideal for mass planting, drifts, raised beds, in the front to middle of mixed perennial borders, in rock gardens or naturalistic gardens.

Form

Multibranched, mounding herbaceous perennial.

Native Range of Species

This selection is of complex hybrid origin; a detailed description of the breeding record can be found in the *Bulletin of the American Penstemon Society* 57, no. 2 (1998): 2–11.

Characteristics

Flowers: Tubular, inflated from near the base, two-lipped, to 1 inch long, borne in leaf axils, vivid violet-purple with white throat, June to August.
Leaves: Opposite, linear-lanceolate, to 2 inches long, without hairs, margins finely toothed, dark green, lustrous.
Stems: Erect, wiry, from woody caudex, without hairs.
Fruits: Capsules.

Culture

Exposure: Full sun to partial shade.
Soil: Garden loam.
Soil Moisture: Moderate watering.
Hardiness: USDA zones 4b to 8.
Elevation Range: Up to 7,000 feet.

Best Features

Compact habit, beautiful flower color, long flowering season.

Disadvantages

Stems become floppy with excessive water. This penstemon benefits from periodic pruning.

Miscellaneous

Plants can be propagated from seeds or stem cuttings taken from nonflowering plants. Cuttings yield the most consistent plants.

Penstemon ×mexicali
Red Rocks penstemon

Periodic pruning and moderate watering will keep Red Rocks penstemon upright and blooming continuously.

Pronunciation: **PEN-steh-mon MEX-ih-cal-ee**

Family: **Scrophulariaceae – figwort family**

Type of Plant: **Herbaceous perennial**

Height: **15 to 18 inches**

Spread: **10 to 15 inches**

Year Introduced: **1999**

Why Chosen

The trademark name of this rosy red sister hybrid to PIKES PEAK PURPLE penstemon commemorates the spectacular outdoor amphitheater near Denver as well as the red rock country of the American West, where penstemons abound. Its repeat blooming habit is extraordinary among hardy penstemons, as is its tolerance of a wide variety of soils and sun exposures. Ray Daugherty selected this color variant at Green Acres Nursery (Golden, Colorado), grown from Bruce Meyers's seeds. Sadly, Meyers, who hybridized the *P. ×mexicali* complex, died before these outstanding plants were introduced. His legacy commemorates the extraordinary work performed by amateur plant hybridizers.

The flowers of many companion plants will come and go throughout the summer, while RED ROCKS penstemon blooms steadfastly.

Landscape Use

Suitable for mass planting, drifts, raised beds, in the front to middle of mixed perennial borders, rock gardens, or naturalistic gardens.

Form

Multibranched, mounding herbaceous perennial.

Native Range of Species

This selection is of complex hybrid origin; a detailed description of the breeding record can be found in the *Bulletin of the American Penstemon Society* 57, no. 2 (1998): 2–11.

Characteristics

Flowers: Tubular, inflated from near the base, two-lipped, to 1 inch long, borne in leaf axils, bright rosy red with white throat, June to August.
Leaves: Opposite, linear-lanceolate, to 2 inches long, without hairs, margins finely toothed, dark green, lustrous.
Stems: Erect, wiry, from woody caudex, without hairs.
Fruits: Capsules.

Culture

Exposure: Full sun to partial shade.
Soil: Garden loam.
Soil Moisture: Moderate watering.
Hardiness: USDA zones 4b to 8.
Elevation Range: Up to 7,000 feet.

Best Features

Compact habit, beautiful flower color, long flowering season.

Disadvantages

Stems become floppy with excessive water. This penstemon benefits from periodic pruning. Reseeds modestly.

Miscellaneous

Plants can be propagated from seeds or stem cuttings taken from nonflowering plants. Cuttings yield the most consistent plants.

Penstemon ×mexicali 'Psmeyers'

SHADOW MOUNTAIN penstemon

SHADOW MOUNTAIN penstemon stays sturdy and erect with infrequent but thorough watering.

Pronunciation: **PEN-steh-mon MEX-ih-cal-ee**

Family: **Scrophulariaceae – figwort family**

Type of Plant: **Herbaceous perennial**

Height: **18 to 24 inches**

Spread: **15 to 18 inches**

Year Introduced: **2007**

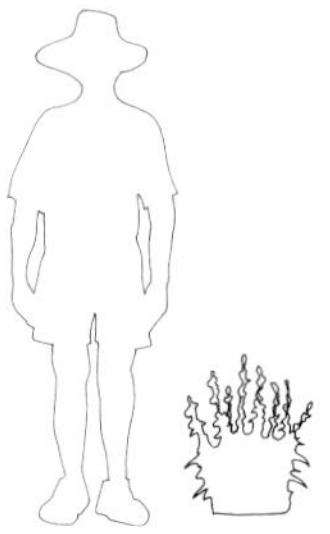

Why Chosen

SHADOW MOUNTAIN penstemon is a sport of PIKES PEAK PURPLE penstemon discovered at Welby Gardens Westwoods (Arvada, Colorado). Its stunningly luminous white-throated lavender-blue flowers are set aglow with distinctive purple-red veining inside the lower throat. Just like its cousins RED ROCKS penstemon and PIKES PEAK PURPLE penstemon, it produces an abundance of colorful flower spikes above mounds of attractive glossy, narrow green leaves from May to September. Although this penstemon performs well in xeric situations, it will produce more flowers over a longer period with moderate watering. The evergreen habit will have a fresh appearance if pruned back each spring.

Flowers are subtle, although they are plentiful and long-lasting.

Landscape Use

Well suited to mass planting, drifts, raised beds, the middle of a mixed perennial border, rock gardens, or naturalistic gardens.

Form

Multibranched, mounding herbaceous perennial.

Native Range of Species

This selection is of complex hybrid origin; a detailed description of the breeding record can be found in the *Bulletin of the American Penstemon Society* 57, no. 2 (1998): 2–11.

Characteristics

Flowers: Tubular, inflated from near the base, two-lipped, to 1 inch long, borne in leaf axils, lavender-blue, throat white with purple-red lines, May to September.
Leaves: Opposite, linear-lanceolate, to 2 inches long, without hairs, margins finely toothed, dark green, lustrous.
Stems: Erect, wiry, from woody caudex, without hairs.
Fruits: Capsules.

Culture

Exposure: Full sun to partial shade.
Soil: Garden loam, clay, or sandy soil.
Soil Moisture: Moderate watering to xeric, once established.
Hardiness: USDA zones 4b to 8.
Elevation Range: Up to 7,000 feet.

Best Features

Compact habit, appealing flower color, long flowering season.

Disadvantages

It is best to avoid frequent heavy watering, which causes stems to become weak and floppy.

Miscellaneous

Plants can be propagated from seeds or stem cuttings taken from nonflowering plants. Cuttings yield the most consistent plants.

Previously listed as 'Psmyers' by Plant Select.

Phlomis cashmeriana Royle ex Benth.

Cashmere sage

Cashmere sage is simply beautiful as a background plant in a perennial border.

Pronunciation: **FLOW-miss cash-mer-ee-ANN-ah**

Family: **Lamiaceae – mint family**

Type of Plant: **Herbaceous perennial**

Height: **36 to 60 inches**

Spread: **18 to 30 inches**

Published: *Hooker's Journal of Botany and Kew Gardens Miscellany* 3: 382. 1833.

Year Recommended: **2004**

Why Chosen

The large, heavily textured leaves, covered with white woolly hairs, form a basal rosette from which the flower stalks emerge in early summer. Each unbranched flower stalk is comprised of verticillasters (false whorls), much like the better-known bee-balm (*Monarda didyma*). The two-lipped lavender-pink flowers open successively from the lowest whorl upward. Refrain from deadheading the unusual flower stalks, because they are architecturally interesting and remain so well into the winter. Left alone, this plant will multiply into a showstopping clump. As the scientific name implies, this plant is native to Kashmir—as well as the rocky slopes of Afghanistan and Pakistan.

Its winter form is just as intriguing as the summer form is eye-catching.

Landscape Use

Excellent as an accent plant, in small groupings, or as a background border plant.

Form

Low-mounding basal rosettes of leaves support erect, elongated flower stalks.

Native Range of Species

Kashmir, Afghanistan, Pakistan, and Turkmenistan; on rocky slopes; 3,600 to 8,000 feet.

Characteristics

Flowers: Tubular, two-lipped, lavender-pink, to 1⅛ inches long, borne in two- to three-whorled spikes that are many-flowered and covered densely with woolly hairs that rub off easily, early summer.

Leaves: Opposite, basal oblong-lanceolate to 7 inches long, stem leaves smaller, margins somewhat shallowly round-toothed, light green, covered densely with woolly hairs, persistent into winter.

Stems: Stout, square, covered densely with white woolly hairs to nearly hairless.

Fruits: Four nutlets.

Culture

Exposure: Full sun to partial shade.
Soil: Garden loam, clay, or sandy soil.
Soil Moisture: Moderate watering in sun to dry shade.
Hardiness: USDA zones 4b to 8.
Elevation Range: Up to 7,000 feet.

Best Features

Unusual flower stalks are architecturally interesting and remain so into the winter. Tolerates clay soils. Use flowering stems in fresh floral arrangements or dried stems in fall arrangements. Cashmere sage is not invasive like other members of the mint family; it will spread slowly.

Disadvantages

Plants don't begin blooming until the second year after planting.

Miscellaneous

These plants are grown from seeds that germinate best when sown after a thirty-day cold stratification period.

Silver sage

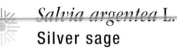

Remove silver sage's flower stems shortly after the flowers have waned to maintain the robust rosette of leaves.

Pronunciation: **SAL-vee-ah ar-GEN-tee-ah**

Family: **Lamiaceae – mint family**

Type of Plant: **Herbaceous perennial**

Height: **24 to 36 inches**

Spread: **12 to 24 inches**

Published: ***Species Plantarum*** **ed. 2, 1: 38. 1762.**

Year Recommended: **1997**

Why Chosen

Although the giant-leaved silver sage has technically been in cultivation for 100 years or more, there was not a single nursery in the United States selling it in the 1990s when it was recommended by Plant Select. Few garden perennials have leaves as massive or showy, like rhubarb wearing an ermine coat. The yard-tall spires of shimmering white flowers are quite striking in the early summer. Cut them back after flowering to stimulate formation of new downy-leaved rosettes. Plants have been known to persist for nearly two decades in the Denver area. Mrs. J. V. Petersen (Littleton, Colorado) provided the original germplasm, subsequently improved by Bluebird Nursery (Clarkson, Nebraska).

The leaves intermingled with hyssop provide unbeatable eye-appeal.

Silver sage's flowers are spectacular when backlit.

Landscape Use

Attractive as an accent plant, in small groupings, for xeriscapes, in rock gardens, as part of dry perennial borders, or in raised planters.

Form

Prostrate basal rosette of leaves with candelabra-like flower stems.

Native Range of Species

Southern Europe to northwestern Africa, into eastern Mediterranean; on limestone and igneous slopes and rock ledges with *Pinus*; 1,000 to 7,860 feet.

Characteristics

Flowers: Tubular, upper lip strongly hooded and lilac, lower lip with a small basal lobe and cream or white, borne in four- to eight-flowered verticillasters, early summer.
Leaves: Opposite, ovate to oblong, mostly basal, margins irregularly jagged, covered with dense, coarse hairs, blades to 10 inches long.
Stems: Flower stems candelabra-like, densely covered with long, soft hairs.
Fruits: Four nutlets.

Culture

Exposure: Full sun to partial shade.
Soil: Average garden soil (easy in almost any good soil).
Soil Moisture: Average to dry, not too wet.
Hardiness: USDA zones 4a to 10.
Elevation Range: Up to 8,000 feet.

Best Features

Architectural flower stems, textural rosettes of woolly leaves.

Disadvantages

Leafy rosettes tend to diminish rather quickly if the flower stems are not removed when blooming ceases. Plants can be short-lived when they receive too much water.

Miscellaneous

Plants are grown from seeds. Don't cover them, as they need light to germinate.

Salvia argentea 93

Salvia darcyi J. Compton 'Pscarl'

VERMILION BLUFFS Mexican sage

Pronunciation: **SAL-vee-ah DAR-see-eye**

Family: **Lamiaceae – mint family**

Type of Plant: **Herbaceous perennial**

Height: **35 to 40 inches**

Spread: **20 to 30 inches**

Published: ***Kew Magazine*** **11(2): 53. 1994.**
 (for the species)

Year Introduced: **2007**

Ann A. Fleming

Why Chosen

Salvia darcyi was collected by John Fairey and Carl Schoenfeld in the Sierra Madre Oriental in Mexico, and they introduced it into commerce at Yucca Do Nursery in Hempstead, Texas. British botanist William D'Arcy is commemorated in the species' name by botanist James Compton, both of whom participated in a collecting trip with Fairey and Schoenfeld in 1991. This sage produces unbeatable brilliant red flowers in widely spaced false whorls from August through October. Hummingbirds can't resist them. The triangular, pastel green leaves are produced in abundance, creating a wonderful foil for the flowers. It spreads slowly by stolons but is quite easily kept in check.

For a fiery display in August, try Vermilion Bluffs Mexican sage.

Landscape Use

Lovely as mass planting or an accent, in the middle or back of borders, in raised planters or rock gardens.

Form

Multibranched, open, and airy mounding perennial.

Native Range of Species

Endemic to the eastern range of the Sierra Madre Oriental in northeastern Mexico (Nuevo León); in rich loam among limestone rocks and boulders; 9,200 feet; rare.

Characteristics

Flowers: Corolla tube, two-lipped, upper lip slightly hooded, brilliant cardinal red, borne three to six per verticillaster widely spaced along the flower stem, August to October.
Leaves: Opposite, deltoid, margins shallowly round-toothed, pastel green, covered with sticky white hairs above and below.
Stems: Woody below, tinged reddish purple with sticky white hairs above.
Fruits: Four nutlets.
Roots: Stoloniferous.

Culture

Exposure: Full sun to partial shade.
Soil: Performs best in loamy soil.
Soil Moisture: Moderate watering.
Hardiness: USDA zones 5b to 10.
Elevation Range: Up to 5,500 feet.

Best Features

Brilliant cardinal red flowers, pastel green foliage, late summer color.

Disadvantages

Does not perform well in poorly drained soils.

Miscellaneous

These plants need to be grown from stem cuttings or divisions. The Plant Select variety has been selected for hardiness.

Irresistible to hummingbirds.

Salvia greggii A. Gray
Wild thing sage

Wild thing sage is arresting when it begins blooming in May.

Pronunciation: **SAL-vee-ah GREG-ee-eye**

Family: **Lamiaceae – mint family**

Type of Plant: **Herbaceous perennial**

Height: **16 to 20 inches**

Spread: **12 to 14 inches**

Published: ***Proceedings of the American Academy of Arts and Sciences* 8: 369. 1870. (for the species)**

Year Introduced: **2005**

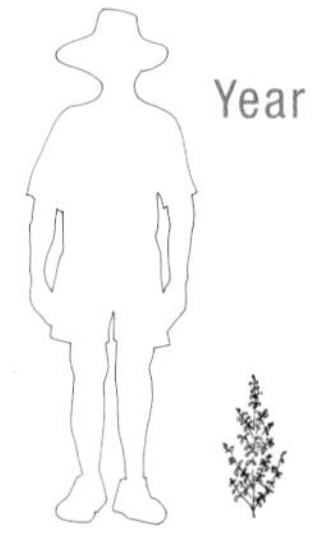

Susan Halstedt

Why Chosen

The species is named for Josiah Gregg, who collected *Salvia greggii* in Mexico in the first half of the 1800s. Germplasm for this particular promotion was acquired by Denver Botanic Gardens from Timberline Gardens (Arvada, Colorado) by Tom Peace. Its shrubby growth habit is open and sports bountiful hot-pink to magenta flowers. It is easy to grow and requires minimal care or supplemental water once established. This drought-tolerant salvia will reward you with a long season of flowers from late spring through early fall. The hot-pink flowers of this selection differ from the scarlet color typical of the species.

Wild thing sage's hot-pink to magenta blossoms are stunning from May to October.

Landscape Use

Ideal as accent plants or massed, in the middle of a perennial border, for rock gardens, or in butterfly and hummingbird gardens.

Form

Mounding, multibranched, shrubby perennial.

Native Range of Species

Central, western, and southern Texas, into north-central Mexico; in rocky soils in pine-oak communities; 4,900 to 8,500 feet.

Characteristics

Flowers: Corolla two-lipped, lower larger and showy, to 1 inch long, hot-pink to magenta, nectariferous, borne sparsely in racemes, May to October.
Leaves: Opposite, obovate to elliptic, to 1 inch long, mostly entire, leathery, without hairs.
Stems: Woody below, erect, multi-branched, mostly without hairs to somewhat covered with minute, soft straight hairs.
Fruits: Four nutlets.

Culture

Exposure: Full sun to partial shade.
Soil: Garden loam, clay, or sandy soil.
Soil Moisture: Moderate watering to xeric.
Hardiness: USDA zones 5b to 10.
Elevation Range: Up to 6,000 feet.

Best Features

Versatile garden performer tolerating dry situations. Hot-pink to magenta flowers. A cornerstone for hummingbird and butterfly gardens.

Disadvantages

Requires moderate protection to overwinter successfully.

Miscellaneous

These plants are produced from stem cuttings, which root easily.

Flower nectar is extremely attractive to hummingbirds and butterflies.

Salvia is an Old Latin name from *salvare*, which means "to heal or save," referring to the medicinal properties of this group of plants.

Salvia greggii A. Gray 'Furman's Red'
Furman's Red sage

Nectar-loving creatures such
as butterflies, hawk moths, and
hummingbirds flock to Furman's Red
sage.

Pronunciation: **SAL-vee-ah GREG-ee-eye**

Family: **Lamiaceae – mint family**

Type of Plant: **Herbaceous perennial**

Height: **18 to 24 inches**

Spread: **12 to 24 inches**

Publication: ***Proceedings of the American Academy of
Arts and Sciences* 8: 369. 1870.**
(for the species, not the cultivar)

Year Recommended: **2005**

Sharon Z. Garrett

Why Chosen

This cultivar was selected by noted Texas plantsman W. A. Furman in the 1970s. 'Furman's Red' is a distinctively compact, upright selection with luxuriantly rich crimson to scarlet flowers that are produced from June to October. As with the typical *Salvia greggii*, its leaves are somewhat leathery. This cultivar is easy to grow and requires minimal care or supplemental water once established. Like wild thing sage, it is valued as a nectar source for hummingbirds and butterflies. Often used as a cornerstone for hummingbird gardens, a grouping of several plants en masse will surely attract hummingbirds.

Landscape Use

Suitable as accent plants or massed, in the middle of a perennial border, in rock gardens, and in butterfly and hummingbird gardens.

Form

Mounding, multibranched, shrubby perennial.

Native Range of Species

Central, western, and southern Texas into north-central Mexico; in rocky soils in pine-oak communities; 4,900 to 8,500 feet.

Late in the summer, when flowers are not as profuse, Furman's Red sage is still an outstanding companion to ORANGE CARPET hummingbird trumpet and ornamental grasses.

Characteristics

Flowers: Corolla two-lipped, lower larger and showy, to 1 inch long, crimson to scarlet, nectariferous, borne sparsely in racemes from June to October.
Leaves: Opposite, obovate to elliptic, to 1 inch long, mostly entire, leathery, without hairs.
Stems: Woody below, erect, multibranched, mostly without hairs to somewhat covered with minute, soft straight hairs.
Fruits: Four nutlets.

Culture

Exposure: Full sun to partial shade.
Soil: Garden loam, clay, or sandy soil.
Soil Moisture: Moderate watering to xeric.
Hardiness: USDA zones 5b to 10.
Elevation Range: Up to 5,500 feet.

Best Features

Versatile garden performer tolerating dry situations. Crimson to scarlet flowers. A cornerstone for hummingbird and butterfly gardens.

Disadvantages

Needs to be planted in a protected site to overwinter, especially on the eastern plains.

Miscellaneous

These plants are produced from stem cuttings, which root easily.

Flower nectar is extremely attractive to hummingbirds, hawk moths, and butterflies.

Salvia is an Old Latin name from *salvare*, which means "to heal or save," referring to the medicinal properties of this group of plants.

Salvia pachyphylla Epling ex Munz
Mojave sage

Mojave sage adds striking structure to a sunny, low-water garden.

Pronunciation: **SAL-vee-ah PACK-ee-fill-ah**

Family: **Lamiaceae – mint family**

Type of Plant: **Herbaceous perennial**

Height: **18 to 36 inches**

Spread: **24 to 36 inches**

Published: ***A Manual of Southern California Botany** 445, 600. 1935.*

Year Recommended: **2005**

Why Chosen

Mojave sage grows to 36 inches or more in the garden, with a width of at least the same dimension. An outstanding feature of this sage is its beautiful, intensely aromatic, silvery green foliage that is covered densely with short, soft hairs. The delicate violet-blue flowers are carried on interrupted spikes of densely whorled bracts that are a lovely smoky mauve-purple. This subshrubby perennial grows best in full-sun locations, with good drainage being essential. The semi-evergreen foliage adds wonderful winter interest to any garden.

Denver Botanic Gardens acquired Mojave sage seeds from Alplains (Kiowa, Colorado), which originally collected the seeds in the Kingston Mountains of California.

Late in the season, the smoky mauve-purple calices fade to brown and provide a subdued contrast to the foliage.

Mojave sage's flowers are a delicate violet-blue early in the season.

Landscape Use

Integrates beautifully as an accent plant, in small groupings to drifts, in the middle of a perennial border, among rocks and boulders, and in rock gardens.

Form

Mounding perennial.

Native Range of Species

Northern Arizona, Southern California, and Baja California; on eroded slopes, upper chaparral to pine forests; 5,000 to 8,500 feet.

Characteristics

Flowers: Tubular, two-lipped, ⅝ to ⅞ inch long, violet-blue, borne in verticillasters of smoky mauve-purple calices, interrupted along spikes, June to November.
Leaves: Opposite, obovate, entire, covered with gray, downy hairs to densely woolly, to 2 to 3 inches long, leathery, resinous, intensely aromatic, semi-evergreen.
Stems: Woody at base with herbaceous new shoots.
Fruits: Four nutlets.

Culture

Exposure: Full sun.
Soil: Well-drained loam or sandy soil.
Soil Moisture: Moderate watering to xeric.
Hardiness: USDA zones 5 to 10.
Elevation Range: Up to 5,500 feet.

Best Features

Very long flowering season. Striking flower and calyx colors. Drought tolerant.

Disadvantages

Dry conditions are a must for successful overwintering. Becomes very woody if not pruned severely each fall after flowering stops. Strong fragrance from the foliage is offensive to some.

Miscellaneous

This plant is typically grown from seeds that require light to germinate. Cuttings are a viable alternative means of propagation, but excess water will cause them to deteriorate.

Seseli gummiferum Pall. ex Smith
Moon carrot

During its first year, moon carrot's basal rosettes of lacy leaves add elegance to the garden.

Pronunciation: **SES-eh-lee gum-MIF-er-um**

Family: **Apiaceae – carrot family**

Type of Plant: **Biennial or short-lived perennial**

Height: **24 to 36 inches**

Spread: **10 to 15 inches**

Published: *Exotic Botany* **2: 121. 1807.**

Year Recommended: **2005**

Melissa L. Martin

Why Chosen

The common name, moon carrot, evokes an image that is hard to resist. Its silvery blue lacy foliage is covered densely with short, soft hairs. As is typical with biennials, the plant forms a basal rosette of leaves the first year. A substantial flower stalk is produced the second year, bearing many pale pink flowers clustered in large, flat umbels. Blooms are continuous and generous from midsummer through fall. Denver Botanic Gardens acquired the original seed lot of this species from a botanical garden in Europe. The species' name is derived from the Latin word for gum, referring to the yellowish, aromatic resin exuded by the flowering stalks.

Flower umbels emerge pink, then fade to white. Despite its delicate appearance, moon carrot is a durable plant that doesn't require much pampering.

Landscape Use

Striking as an architectural accent, in mixed dry borders, in containers and planters, and in dry rock gardens.

Form

Basal rosettes are produced the first year; stout, upright succulent stems form an erect to slightly sprawling mound in the second year.

Native Range of Species

South Aegean region and into Bulgaria; on limestone cliffs; below 3,275 feet.

Characteristics

Flowers: Pale pink flowers clustered in large, flat umbels to 2 inches across, midsummer to fall.

Leaves: Alternate, finely two- to three-pinnate, to 6 inches long, silvery blue in basal rosettes.

Stems: Erect to reclining with ascending tips, stout, succulent, bluish, without hairs to covered densely with short, soft hairs, with smaller leaves above.

Fruits: Schizocarp of two mericarps.

Culture

Exposure: Full sun to partial shade.
Soil: Garden loam, clay, or sandy soil.
Soil Moisture: Moderate watering to xeric.
Hardiness: USDA zones 5 to 9.
Elevation Range: Up to 5,000 feet.

Best Features

Moon carrot is easy to grow in either full sun or part shade and is not fussy about soils. It can adapt to moderate or low watering regimes.

Disadvantages

Moon carrot is a biennial. Allow plants to produce seeds, then harvest or allow to self-sow for future garden displays. Reseeding may be locally abundant, and seedlings may require thinning.

Miscellaneous

Plants are grown from seeds that will germinate readily without pretreatment.

Spartina pectinata Link
Prairie cordgrass

Pronunciation: **spar-TEEN-ah peck-tin-AH-tah**

Family: **Poaceae – grass family**

Type of Plant: **Perennial ornamental grass**

Height: **20 to 36 inches**

Spread: **20 to 30 inches**

Published: *Jahrbücher der Gewächskunde* 1(3): 92. 1820.

Year Recommended: **1999**

Why Chosen

Prairie cordgrass is a native grass found across much of North America in moist swales and wet prairies. Plant Select does not recommend growing it in conventional garden settings due to its widely spreading root system. Confined in rich, heavy clay in a container, however, this grass makes a stunning specimen in a water garden. The slower stems can rise to 36 inches or more by summer's end, and the entire plant turns a brilliant yellow color that glows when backlit, well into the depths of winter. The species' name refers to the pectinate, or comblike, appearance of the spikelets.

Landscape Use

Best used as a contained aquatic plant for ponds, lakes, or along the edges of marshes or sloughs.

Form

Densely tufted, mostly erect to somewhat spreading, rhizomatous grass.

Native Range of Species

Extremely widespread throughout the northeastern quarter of the United States and north into Canada, through the Great Plains to Texas and New Mexico, with scattered populations in the Pacific Northwest. Grows in both wet and dry soils, including marshes and sloughs to dry prairies and disturbed areas along roads and railroad rights-of-way.

There is nothing more visually gratifying than a combination of sunlight, water, and prairie cordgrass.

Characteristics

Flowers: Borne in panicles 4 to 20 inches long, five to fifty branches, lying flat to spreading with ten to eighty spikelets, midsummer to fall.
Leaves: Alternate, blades 24 to 36 inches long, flat, mostly without hairs, margins rough to the touch, brilliant yellow into winter.
Stems: Stout and wiry, forming clumps, without hairs, 20 to 36 inches (when grown in water).
Roots: Rhizomatous.

Culture

Exposure: Full sun to partial shade.
Soil: Best planted in heavy clay loam.
Soil Moisture: Best submerged in 1 to 6 inches of water.
Hardiness: USDA zones 4 to 8.
Elevation Range: Up to 8,000 feet.

Best Features

Very adaptable to various soil types and moisture levels. Phenomenal fall and winter color.

Disadvantages

Can spread somewhat aggressively from well-developed rhizomes. Best used in containers for aquatic display. Basal culm sheaths reported to be persistent and spinelike; caution is advised when working with older plants.

Miscellaneous

These plants can be grown from seeds or divisions. Divide plants when they are actively growing and allow a few weeks for them to reestablish. Keep newly planted divisions moderately moist until they become established. Potted plants can be heeled into the garden for winter.

Soil conservation agencies have used this grass to control erosion and as a rejuvenator in wetlands and prairies.

Native Americans used this species as thatch on earth-covered lodges in their permanent villages.

Sporobolus wrightii Munro ex Scribn.
Giant sacaton

Leave plenty of room for this beauty's elegant natural form.

Pronunciation: **spo-RAH-boh-lus WRIGHT-ee-eye**

Family: **Poaceae – grass family**

Type of Plant: **Perennial ornamental grass**

Height: **60 to 72 inches**

Spread: **36 to 60 inches**

Published: ***Bulletin of the Torrey Botanical Club* 9: 103. 1882.**

Year Recommended: **2006**

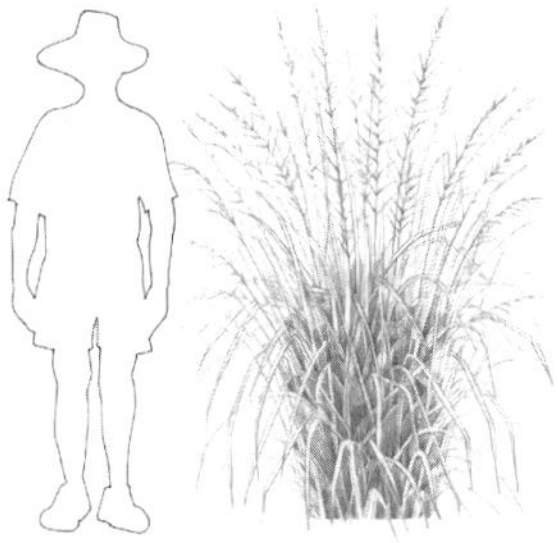

Why Chosen

Giant sacaton is a wonderful xeric grass native to the Southwest and south into Mexico. Flowering culms, produced in late summer, can easily reach 6 feet in height. The sturdy panicles of flowers produce reddish brown seeds and ultimately become golden and wispy. This beautiful plant can ultimately reach 5 feet wide, adding impressive structure to your garden. The leaves turn a lovely golden color in fall, providing winter interest. Giant sacaton is very drought tolerant but performs best with a couple of deep waterings during the driest months. Its stature makes it a great alternative for other nonnative water-loving grasses such as maiden grass.

Landscape Use

Striking as an accent plant, in mass plantings, borders, ornamental grass designs, naturalistic gardens, on slopes and hillsides.

Form

Densely tufted, erect to gracefully spreading mound.

Native Range of Species

Arkansas west to Arizona, south to north-central Mexico; on moist clay flats and rocky slopes near saline habitats; 1,000 to 6,800 feet.

Giant sacaton's tall, arching stems support long flower panicles that add grace to a garden path.

Characteristics

Flowers: Borne in panicles, 8 to 24 inches long, open-spreading, lowest branches to 4 inches long, late summer to fall.
Leaves: Alternate, blades 8 to 28 inches long, flat, margins rough to the touch, without hairs beneath, golden color from fall to winter.
Stems: Stout, 3 to 7 feet tall.
Fruits: Achene, elliptic, reddish brown or blackish.
Roots: Caespitose.

Culture

Exposure: Full sun to partial shade.
Soil: Garden loam, clay, or sandy soil.
Soil Moisture: Moderate watering to very dry.
Hardiness: USDA zones 5 to 8.
Elevation Range: Up to 7,000 feet.

Best Features

Graceful, spreading mound. Glowing color from leaves and panicles in fall and winter, especially when backlit by the sun. The inflorescences can be used in fresh and dried arrangements, a nice addition for fall and winter decorating.

Disadvantages

Old culms must be cut to the ground in early spring to maintain unencumbered symmetrical habit.

Miscellaneous

Plants are grown from seeds that germinate readily with no pretreatments.

Soil conservation agencies use this species for erosion control and revegetation.

The plants provide forage and cover protection for animals, and the seeds are eaten by some birds.

Native Americans ground the seeds alone or with cornmeal to make mush or bread, and they bound the stiff stems into brushes.

Sporobolus wrightii 107

Turkish veronica.

Perennial Groundcovers

Clockwise from top:
winecups, winecups,
TABLE MOUNTAIN ice plant.

Sea Foam artemisia

Sea Foam artemisia's frothy leaf texture gives the plant its name.

Pronunciation: **ar-tem-EE-see-ah VER-sih-cull-er**

Family: **Asteraceae – sunflower family**

Type of Plant: **Herbaceous perennial**

Height: **6 to 12 inches**

Spread: **18 to 30 inches**

Year Recommended: **2004**

Karla Beatty

Why Chosen

Like the frothy tip of a crashing wave, the feathery, filigreed foliage of *Artemisia versicolor* 'Sea Foam' adds a beautiful and unique texture to the garden. The low-growing, somewhat spreading habit of this plant makes it an attractive choice for planting along rock walls, as it will spill and drape over the edge. The spreading habit of growth makes it a perfect choice for an attractive groundcover in hot, dry areas. It is highly tolerant of poor, dry soil conditions and prefers good drainage to maintain the highly curled and silver attributes. *Artemisia versicolor* 'Sea Foam' was originally recommended to Plant Select by Lauren Springer Ogden, author of *The Undaunted Garden*.

Nestled between the rich green of yellow ice plant and dark green leaves of mock bearberry, Sea Foam artemisia shows off its contrasting color and texture.

Landscape Use

Nice accent in a dry border, as groundcover, in drift or mass plantings. Attractive when planted along rock walls where it can cascade and drape, among rocks and boulders, along walkway edges, or in naturalistic areas.

Form

The spreading habit of growth makes this plant a great groundcover in hot, dry areas.

Native Range of Species

This selection is thought to be a member of the "vulgares" group in *Artemisia* subgenus *Artemisia*, a conglomerate of New World and Old World species that is not readily subdivided.

Characteristics

Flowers: Greenish white, insignificant, April to June, scattered flowering later.
Leaves: Alternate, silvery blue, lacy and feathery, mounding, year-round appeal.
Stems: Gently curved and twisted, semiwoody.
Fruits: Achenes.

Culture

Exposure: Full sun to partial shade.
Soil: Garden loam, clay, or sandy soil.
Soil Moisture: Moderate watering to dry.
Hardiness: USDA zones 3 to 9.
Elevation Range: Up to 7,000 feet.

Best Features

The curlicuing silvery blue foliage stands in unique contrast to typical artemisias. 'Sea Foam' generally doesn't exhibit the middle-of-the-plant meltdown characteristic often seen in other artemisias, giving it a better winter presence. It is highly tolerant of poor, dry soil conditions.

Disadvantages

Overwatering may cause leaf necrosis and stem dieback. The strong, compact form is best maintained by severe pruning in the late fall.

Miscellaneous

Cuttings taken before flowering root best when subirrigated; excessive overhead watering during rooting will cause leaves to deteriorate.

Callirhoe involucrata (Torr. & A. Gray) A. Gray
Winecups

Winecups is a native western plant that performs best with little supplemental water.

Pronunciation: **cal-lih-ROW-ee in-vol-you-CRAY-tah**

Family: **Malvaceae – mallow family**

Type of Plant: **Herbaceous perennial**

Height: **5 to 8 inches**

Spread: **20 to 30 inches**

Published: *Memoirs of the American Academy of Arts and Science, new series (II).* **4: 16. 1849.**

Year Recommended: **1999**

Why Chosen

This showy native resembles a compact, prostrate geranium and is both versatile and durable. Its most obvious attraction is the continuous succession of cup-shaped flowers in a rich wine red color with a distinctive white eye; flowers appear from late spring through the summer. The lustrous dark blue-green palmate leaves are attractive in their own right, even taking on fine reddish tints in the autumn. Once established, it forms a long, stout taproot and will thrive even with no supplemental irrigation. It is one incredibly durable plant!

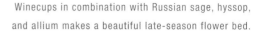
Winecups in combination with Russian sage, hyssop, and allium makes a beautiful late-season flower bed.

This groundcover flowers from spring until fall.

Landscape Use

Suitable as a groundcover or in combination with perennials or annuals along the edge of raised beds or walls. Its trailing stems weave well among companion plants or cascade over walls, boulders, and slopes. A natural for short- to midgrass meadows.

Form

Low mat of 1- to 3-foot-long trailing stems.

Native Range of Species

Minnesota to Utah, south to Texas and New Mexico; dry plains; 3,500 to 6,000 feet.

Characteristics

Flowers: Cup shaped with five slightly recurved petals, wine red to magenta fading to purple with white centers, to 2½ inches across, April to hard frost.
Leaves: Alternate, palmately lobed, five- to seven-divided nearly to the base, rounded in overall outline, rich dark blue-green.
Stems: Sturdy, procumbent.
Fruits: Hardened, flattened, and discoid.
Roots: Deep taproots, thick and mealy.

Culture

Exposure: Full sun to partial shade.
Soil: Average garden soil.
Soil Moisture: Moderate watering to dry.
Hardiness: USDA zones 3 to 9.
Elevation Range: Up to 8,000 feet.

Best Features

Long season of bloom.

Disadvantages

Overwatering causes the stems to become straggly and collapse, exposing the crown of the plant. May be slow to emerge from dormancy in spring. Requires a generous amount of space to spread out.

Miscellaneous

Callirhoe produce prodigious numbers of seeds, each with an impervious seed coat and held inside a protective capsule; both are protective adaptations against fire in its native habitat. Treating seeds with gibberellic acid aids germination. Mechanical or chemical scarification is effective but has drawbacks. Primed seeds germinate most successfully.

Delosperma dyeri L. Bolus 'Psdold'
RED MOUNTAIN ice plant

RED MOUNTAIN ice plant's flowers fade to a coppery red as they age.

Pronunciation: **del-oh-SPERM-ah DYE-er-eye**

Family: **Aizoaceae – fig-marigold family**

Type of Plant: **Perennial groundcover**

Height: **2 to 3 inches**

Spread: **15 to 20 inches**

Published: *Notes on Mesembryanthemum and Allied Genera Pt. 1*, 135. 1928. (for the species)

Year Introduced: **2007**

Why Chosen

This shocking red-flowered ice plant was selected from seedlings grown from a wild collection made in the Eastern Cape province of South Africa. In nature, the flowers vary from a tawny orange to brilliant vermilion. The flowers of this cultivar open a burnished red color that positively glows, and then they fade to a coppery red. The striking contrast between fresh and aging flowers makes this plant even more alluring. The foliage superficially resembles that of the TABLE MOUNTAIN ice plant, although it is perhaps a bit grayer, with more ruddy highlights. RED MOUNTAIN ice plant is quite compact, spreading a bit more modestly than TABLE MOUNTAIN ice plant. It appears to be somewhat more drought tolerant, but with comparable hardiness.

When first open, flowers are burnished red. Plants remain fairly compact, although they spread slowly as they mature.

Landscape Use

Attractive in small groupings, mass planting, drifts, as the foreground of a perennial border, in trough gardens, among rocks and boulders, draping over walls and boulders, along walkway edges, and in rock gardens.

Form

Mat-forming groundcover perennial.

Native Range of Species

Eastern Cape province, South Africa.

Characteristics

Flowers: Burnished red petals fading to coppery red with a creamy center, to 1 inch across, April to September.
Leaves: Opposite, ovate to ovate-lanceolate, to about ½ inch long and ⅓ inch across, glossy papillose, succulent, year-round appeal.
Stems: Prostrate, spreading.
Fruits: Capsules.

Culture

Exposure: Full sun to partial shade.
Soil: Garden loam, clay, or sandy soil.
Soil Moisture: Moderate watering to xeric once established.
Hardiness: USDA zones 5 to 8.
Elevation Range: Up to 6,000 feet.

Best Features

Distinctive flower color that combines exceptionally well with yellow or blue. Readily forms dense groundcover mats. Roots readily along stems.

Disadvantages

Intolerant of poorly drained soils and foot traffic.

Miscellaneous

Plants are produced from cuttings or divisions. Like the other mat-forming delospermas, stems that touch the ground will root but can be pulled off rather easily and transplanted or potted.

Delosperma floribundum L. Bolus
Starburst ice plant

Long-lasting starburst ice plant flowers are distinctive with their white centers and narrow, intense lilac-pink petals.

Pronunciation: **del-oh-SPERM-ah flor-ee-BUN-dum**

Family: **Aizoaceae – fig-marigold family**

Type of Plant: **Perennial groundcover**

Height: **2 to 4 inches**

Spread: **10 to 12 inches**

Published: ***Notes on Mesembryanthemum and Allied Genera Pt. 1**, 135. 1928.*

Year Introduced: **1998**

Why Chosen

Starburst ice plant, unique among delospermas, was introduced to cultivation by Panayoti Kelaidis of Denver Botanic Gardens. He collected seeds near Springfontein in the Orange Free State province of South Africa in March 1996. Within weeks of sowing the seeds, plants produce compact tufts of succulent foliage and can flower shortly thereafter. The 2-inch flowers are a shimmering lilac-pink with a large white eye, making the flowers utterly distinct from the better-known *D. cooperi*. Unlike the other outstanding delospermas of Plant Select, starburst ice plant is almost shrubby in habit, growing from a distinct taproot with woody aboveground stems that spread a foot or more in length.

Group a variety of ice plants such as starburst (upper right), MESA VERDE (upper left), and purple (bottom) for an eye-catching display.

Landscape Use

Excellent for the foreground of perennial borders, trough gardens, among rocks and boulders, draping over walls and boulders, along walkway edges, and in rock gardens.

Form

Mat-forming groundcover perennial.

Native Range of Species

Cape, Orange Free State, and Natal provinces, South Africa.

Characteristics

Flowers: Shimmering, bright lilac-pink petals with a white center, to 1⅖ inches across, June to frost.
Leaves: Opposite, semicylindrical, long-tapered, minutely papillose, ¾ to 2 inches long, green, succulent, year-round appeal.
Stems: Densely branching, from a woody caudex.
Fruits: Capsules.
Roots: Stout taproots.

Culture

Exposure: Full sun.
Soil: Average garden soil.
Soil Moisture: Moderate watering to dry, not too wet.
Hardiness: USDA zones 4a to 9.
Elevation Range: Up to 8,000 feet.

Best Features

Wide range of climatic tolerance. Performs best in sites that receive full sun throughout the year.

Disadvantages

Intolerant of poorly drained soils and foot traffic.

Miscellaneous

This is one of the delospermas that is easily grown from seeds.

Delosperma N.E. Br. 'John Proffitt'
TABLE MOUNTAIN ice plant

TABLE MOUNTAIN ice plant begins flowering in early spring. It is an ideal complement to rocks in a rock garden.

Pronunciation: **del-oh-SPERM-ah**

Family: **Aizoaceae – fig-marigold family**

Type of Plant: **Perennial groundcover**

Height: **2 to 4 inches**

Spread: **15 to 18 inches**

Year Introduced: **2002**

Why Chosen

Parent seed of this plant was collected by Panayoti Kelaidis in 1996 from a vigorous groundcover found in the foothills of the Drakensberg near Matatiele in the Eastern Cape province. This particularly vigorous and showy strain was selected at Denver Botanic Gardens. The flowers are fuchsia, often with an eye-catching white center. The succulent leaves are somewhat boat-shaped and dark blue-green that flush with a purple tinge during the winter months. The cultivar commemorates John Proffitt, a retired acting director of Denver Botanic Gardens. The trademark name Table Mountain is a tribute to the mesa in Golden, Colorado, and those found throughout South Africa.

The flowers are real showstoppers when in their full glory.

Landscape Use

Suitable as a foreground of a perennial border, to trough gardens, among rocks and boulders, draping over walls and boulders, along walkway edges, and in rock gardens.

Form

Mat-forming groundcover perennial.

Native Range of Species

Eastern Cape province of South Africa.

Characteristics

Flowers: Lustrous fuchsia petals with a white base that give the flowers a white center, to 1½ inches across, spring to fall.
Leaves: Opposite, sessile, succulent, narrow, green leaves that remain turgid in winter, often tinged with purple, to ½ inch long, year-round appeal.
Stems: Prostrate, spreading.
Fruits: Capsules.

Culture

Exposure: Sun to partial shade.
Soil: Clay, loam, or sandy soils.
Soil Moisture: Moderate watering to dry.
Hardiness: USDA zones 4 to 9.
Elevation Range: Up to 7,000 feet.

Best Features

An adaptable plant that thrives in a variety of sites, growing best in amended soil with occasional watering. It is also drought tolerant.

Disadvantages

Intolerant of poorly drained soils and foot traffic.

Miscellaneous

Readily propagated from stem cuttings.

Delosperma N.E. Br. 'Kelaidis'[PP13,876]
Mesa Verde ice plant

You can identify this unique hybrid ice plant by its salmon pink petals and pale yellow center.

Pronunciation: **del-oh-SPERM-ah**

Family: **Aizoaceae – fig-marigold family**

Type of Plant: **Perennial groundcover**

Height: **2 to 4 inches**

Spread: **12 to 15 inches**

Year Introduced: **2002**

Janet Warren

Why Chosen

MESA VERDE ice plant is a spontaneous hybrid between a dwarf high-altitude form of *Delosperma cooperi* and *D. nubigenum* or *D. basuticum*. It appeared in evaluation plots at Denver Botanic Gardens in 1997. The iridescent soft-salmon-pink flowers, produced from summer into autumn, glow with a coppery sheen. Like other hardy ice plants, the succulent leaves hug the ground and extend the display through the winter by turning bronze in color. Due to the high alpine provenance of the parents and the plant's resulting hybrid vigor, MESA VERDE ice plant has proven to be especially adaptable and cold hardy in the maritime climate of Europe and the eastern United States. Ed Snodgrass, nurseryman and author of *Green Roof Plants*, says it is a staple green roof plant of the Atlantic seaboard.

Large plantings of MESA VERDE ice plant are a magnet to garden visitors.

Landscape Use

Best used as the foreground of a perennial border, in trough gardens, among rocks and boulders, draping over walls and boulders, along walkway edges, and in rock gardens.

Form

Mat-forming groundcover perennial.

Native Range of Species

Nativities of the parents are *Delosperma basuticum*: Lesotho province, South Africa; *D. cooperi*: Orange Free State province, South Africa; *D. nubigenum*: Cape and Orange Free State provinces, South Africa.

Characteristics

Flowers: Iridescent salmon pink petals with a pale yellow center, to 1½ inches across, summer into autumn.
Leaves: Opposite, narrow, succulent green leaves, to ½ inch long, year-round apeal.
Stems: Prostrate, spreading.
Fruits: Capsules.

Culture

Exposure: Full sun to partial shade.
Soil: Garden loam, clay to gravelly soils.
Soil Moisture: Moderate watering to drier conditions.
Hardiness: USDA zones 4b to 8.
Elevation Range: Up to 7,000 feet.

Best Features

Distinctive flower color that combines exceptionally well with yellow or blue. MESA VERDE ice plant readily forms dense groundcover mats. It is somewhat more compact in form and less aggressive than *Delosperma cooperi*.

Disadvantages

Intolerant of poorly drained soils and foot traffic.

Miscellaneous

Readily grown from stem cuttings.

Epilobium canum (Greene) P. H. Raven subsp. *garrettii* (A. Nelson) P. H. Raven
ORANGE CARPET hummingbird trumpet

ORANGE CARPET hummingbird trumpet's bright red-orange flowers cascade appealingly over rock walls.

Pronunciation: **ep-ee-LOBE-ee-um KANE-um subspecies gair-RET-tee-eye**

Family: **Onagraceae – evening primrose family**

Type of Plant: **Herbaceous perennial**

Height: **4 to 6 inches**

Spread: **15 to 20 inches**

Published: ***Annals of the Missouri Botanical Garden*** **63(2): 335. 1976. (for subspecies, not selection)**

Year Recommended: **2001**

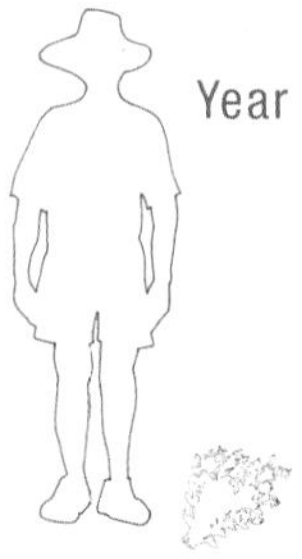

Why Chosen

This hummingbird trumpet forms compact mats of hairy blue-green foliage and has been known to open its first flowers as early as May in some years, but invariably by the Fourth of July. It is also the most moisture- and cold-tolerant species, thriving in most of the continental United States, even in places where many western wildflowers are limited by moisture sensitivity. David Salman selected this compact cultivar at his nursery (Santa Fe Greenhouses, Santa Fe, New Mexico) from seeds collected by Panayoti and Gwen Kelaidis in the foothills near the Wyoming border in easternmost Idaho. The species' name, *canum,* refers to the grayish white hairs covering the leaves, and the subspecies' name, *garrettii,* commemorates its discoverer, A. O. Garrett.

Left: ORANGE CARPET hummingbird trumpet dresses up this sunny, dry, and hot garden.

Right: Flower color can range from red-orange to scarlet.

Landscape Use

Groundcover, ideal for dry locations among rocks, cascading over low walls, on slopes, as a foreground of the perennial border, in rock gardens, and along path edges.

Form

Densely branched, low-growing groundcover.

Native Range of Species

Southeastern Idaho and western Wyoming through Utah and into northwestern Arizona; in scree, rock crevices, and on dry open slopes; 5,240 to 10,150 feet.

Characteristics

Flowers: Funnel form with four notched petals, 1 to 1½ inches long, slightly zygomorphic, borne in short terminal spikes, bright red-orange to scarlet, nectariferous, mid- to late summer

Leaves: Opposite, narrowly elliptic, whitish blue-green, margins minutely serrate, ⅖ to 1⅔ inches long, densely covered with minute, soft, straight glandular hairs.

Stems: Woody at base with herbaceous new shoots, ascending to lax, more or less erect.

Fruits: Slender capsules to about 1 inch long, seeds comose.

Culture

Exposure: Full sun to partial shade.

Soil: Sandy soil or clay loam (not fussy).

Soil Moisture: Moderate watering to dry.

Hardiness: USDA zones 3 to 8.

Elevation Range: Up to 9,000 feet.

Best Features

Bright flower color. Low growth habit. Long flowering season. Very attractive to hummingbirds. Tolerant of dry conditions.

Disadvantages

Susceptible to flea beetles. Needs plenty of room to spread out.

Miscellaneous

This selection is grown from stem cuttings that are taken before plants begin to flower.

Tremendous magnet for hummingbirds.

Previously listed as *Zauschneria garrettii* A. Nelson by Plant Select.

Eriogonum umbellatum Torr. var. *aureum* (Gand.) Reveal 'Psdowns'
KANNAH CREEK buckwheat

KANNAH CREEK buckwheat's flowers are showy during the first half of the growing season.

Pronunciation: ehr-ee-OG-ah-num um-bel-LAY-tum variety OR-ee-um

Family: **Polygonaceae – buckwheat family**

Type of Plant: **Herbaceous perennial**

Height: **12 to 15 inches**

Spread: **12 to 24 inches**

Published: *Taxon* 17(5): 532. 1968.
(for the variety, not the cultivar)

Year Introduced: **2007**

Why Chosen

In the early 1980s, Dermod Downs was hiking along Kannah Creek near Grand Junction, Colorado, when he saw what he thought was an improvement on the typical sulfur flower he'd been growing as propagator of Green Acres Nursery (Golden, Colorado). The plants he grew from cuttings have proven themselves in cultivation for over two decades in the Denver area. The lavish floral display begins in May with umbels of bright yellow flowers and extends to midsummer as the persistent petals age to orange and nearly red. KANNAH CREEK buckwheat forms a low mat of deep green leaves that turn a glowing, vivid purple-red in the winter months.

Left: KANNAH CREEK buckwheat has a beautiful, natural effect when placed informally in a border.

Right: As the flowers and sepals age, their orange-red tint intensifies.

Landscape Use

A great border perennial or groundcover, planted individually for accent, in masses or drifts, among rocks, in the rock garden, or xeriscape.

Form

Low-growing loose mats of foliage.

Native Range of Species

The variety is found on the Western Slope of Colorado near Grand Mesa. It is widespread at middle altitudes.

Characteristics

Flowers: Undifferentiated petals and sepals (tepals) are persistent, sulfur yellow, enlarging with age and becoming orange to nearly red, umbellate or subcapitate on leafless stalks, May to July.

Leaves: Alternate, obovate or spatulate, hairless above and beneath, ⅓ to 1½ inches long, spreading rosettes change from green to a vivid purple-red in winter, year-round appeal.

Stems: Emerge from woody caudex.

Fruits: Three-winged achenes.

Culture

Exposure: Full sun to partial shade.

Soil: Garden loam, clay, or sandy soil.

Soil Moisture: Moderate watering to xeric.

Hardiness: USDA zones 3 to 8.

Elevation Range: Up to 10,000 feet.

Best Features

KANNAH CREEK buckwheat thrives in typical xeric culture but also grows lustily when water is withheld altogether. Foliage is attractive throughout the winter months.

Miscellaneous

Seeds germinate well after a fourteen- to thirty-day cold stratification; do not cover seeds, as they need light to germinate.

Native Americans used various parts of the plant prepared in a variety of manners to treat gonorrheal sores, ptomaine poisoning, biliousness, colds, stomachaches, lameness or rheumatism, lengthy menses, or to soothe pain from burns.

Eriogonum lacks the sheathing stipule (ochrea) that is characteristic of the buckwheat family.

Eriogonum umbellatum var. *aureum* 'Psdowns' 125

Gazania krebsiana Less.
TANAGER gazania

TANAGER gazania produces a gay bouquet in any sunny exposure.

Pronunciation: **gah-ZANE-ee-ah KREB-zee-ann-ah**

Family: **Asteraceae – sunflower family**

Type of Plant: **Herbaceous perennial**

Height: **4 to 6 inches**

Spread: **8 to 12 inches**

Published: *Synopsis Generum Compositarum* 44. 1832. **(for the species, not this orange selection)**

Year Recommended: **2003**

Stephanie Busby

Why Chosen

Kees Sahin (K. Sahin, Zaden B. V., Netherlands) obtained seeds of the typically red-flowered *Gazania krebsiana* from the Kirstenbosch National Botanical Garden in Cape Town, South Africa, in the 1970s and selected atypical orange-flowered plants from the evaluation plants. These were subsequently developed into a uniform strain with flowers 3 inches or more across. TANAGER gazania is a further refinement of this strain that provides a positively shocking orange splash to gardens. The seedlings can be planted outdoors well before the average date of last frost, and they mature into very drought-tolerant plants before summer's end. This species is named for Georg Krebs (1792–1844), a German apothecary and plant collector who traveled in South Africa in 1817.

Flowers open fully in sunlight, but will close with cloud cover or when in shade.

Landscape Use

A perfect plant for rock gardens, the front of a bed or border, in planters, massing, or drifts, or in shortgrass meadows.

Form

Neat, very low-mounding tufted rosettes to mats.

Native Range of Species

Widespread in central and eastern South Africa, east and southern tropical Africa; along seasonal streams, on floodplains, flats, disturbed areas, coastal dunes, and coastal grasslands; from sea level to high elevation.

Characteristics

Flowers: Daisylike heads to 2½ inches across borne singly on leafless stalks to 6 inches long, ray flowers are Day-Glo orange with dramatic basal black spots, spring to fall.
Leaves: Alternate, linear to linear-lanceolate in rosettes, to 6¼ inches long, deeply lobed, margins rolled under, glossy above and hoary beneath, dark green developing a deep purple tinge in winter, year-round appeal.
Stems: Latex is milky.
Fruits: Achenes.
Roots: Upper portion woody.

Culture

Exposure: Full sun to partial shade.
Soil: Loam, sandy or clay soils.
Soil Moisture: Moderate watering to dry.
Hardiness: USDA zones 6 to 10.
Elevation Range: Up to 5,500 feet.

Best Features

Intense orange flower heads. Glossy, dark green foliage.

Disadvantages

Not reliably hardy but can persist in protected microclimates. Reseeds moderately in USDA zone 5.

Miscellaneous

Plants are easily grown from seeds, but avoid keeping seedlings too wet.

Flowers may be eaten raw. Dense hairs from the undersides of the leaves are rolled into twine to make skirts in Lesotho, South Africa. Used traditionally to treat sickly babies, earache, and sterility in women. A popular garden plant that has been in cultivation since 1755.

Gazania linearis (Thunb.) Druce
COLORADO GOLD gazania

COLORADO GOLD gazania is bright and cheery, particularly en masse.

Pronunciation: gah-ZANE-ee-ah lin-ee-AIR-iss

Family: **Asteraceae – sunflower family**

Type of Plant: **Herbaceous perennial**

Height: **3 to 6 inches**

Spread: **8 to 12 inches**

Published: *Report of the Botanical Society and Exchange Club of the British Isles* 4: 624. 1917. (for the species)

Year Introduced: **1998**

Why Chosen

Widespread at the highest elevations in the Drakensberg Mountains of South Africa, this linear-leaved gazania is quite variable from one part of that region to the next. Numerous accessions were grown at Denver Botanic Gardens from collections made all over the Drakensberg in 1994 by Panayoti Kelaidis. Over time, these plants hybridized naturally, yielding this vigorous strain of the hardiest gazania, which often blooms in the heart of winter. Flowers open in sunlight, are produced in abundance through spring, and appear in flushes much of the rest of the year. The species' name describes the extremely linear shape of its leaves.

Left: The hot flower colors of gazania, sweet William, and California poppy make a simple but pleasing combination.

Right: Rock gardens are a perfect setting for this plant.

Landscape Use

Well suited to massing or drifts, a perfect plant for rock gardens, the front of beds or borders, in planters, or in shortgrass meadows.

Form

Low-mounding to mat-forming tufted rosettes.

Native Range of Species

Drakensberg mountain range of Eastern Cape and Natal provinces in South Africa; in open grassland; sea level to about 10,000 feet.

Characteristics

Flowers: Daisylike heads to 2¾ inches across borne on stalks to 12 inches long, ray flowers yellow with black basal spots, February into November.
Leaves: Alternate, linear to linear-lanceolate in rosettes, to 8 inches long, margins rolled under, deep green and without hairs above, covered densely with silvery woolly hairs beneath, persistent through winter, year-round appeal.
Fruits: Achenes.
Roots: Woody in upper portion.

Culture

Exposure: Full sun to partial shade.
Soil: Thrives in garden loam; needs light fertilizing in sandy soils.
Soil Moisture: Moderate watering to dry.
Hardiness: USDA zones 4 to 8.
Elevation Range: Up to 9,000 feet.

Best Features

The narrow, grasslike leaves are evergreen and pleasing in their own right. Long flowering season.

Disadvantages

Self-sows and can be mildly invasive. Seedlings may need thinning from year to year.

Miscellaneous

Plants are readily grown from seeds. Avoid keeping seedlings too wet.

La Veta Lace geranium

Pronunciation: **jer-AIN-ee-um mag-neh-FLOOR-um**

Family: **Geraniaceae – geranium family**

Type of Plant: **Herbaceous perennial**

Height: **6 to 10 inches**

Spread: **18 to 24 inches**

Published: *Botanishe Jahrbücher für Systematic, Pflanzengeschichte und Pflanzengeographie* 40: 68. 1907.

Year Introduced: **2003**

Why Chosen

Seeds of *Geranium magniflorum* were collected by Panayoti Kelaidis (Denver Botanic Gardens) at the base of Joubert's Pass in the Drakensberg Mountains of the Eastern Cape province, South Africa, in 1996. Selected from this germplasm, LA VETA LACE geranium bears striking vivid purple-lilac flowers from late spring to midsummer. Not only do the flowers provide a departure from the rest of the genus, but the foliage is the most finely divided of any hardy geranium, reminiscent of threadlike parsley leaves. *Magniflorum* means "having large flowers," a morphological feature that is atypical for the genus. The name of this plant is often confused with the Himalayan *G. magnificum*, which is much less distinctive.

Landscape Use

Striking when used in massing, drifts, or as a groundcover, in rock gardens, or in the front of the border.

Form

Neat, low-mounding mats of foliage that spread gradually.

Native Range of Species

Central and eastern South Africa; common in moist grasslands to uplands; 7,500 to 9,825 feet.

Characteristics

Flowers: Five-petaled, each cleft, borne in lax terminal clusters, to 1 inch across, vivid purple-lilac, late spring to midsummer.

Leaves: Alternate, digitately divided into five lobes, each lobe bipinnately divided, to 2⅓ inches across, green changing to scarlet or purple into early winter.

Stems: Reclining with ascending tips, pink to reddish early in the growing season, turning green.

Fruits: Long, pointed like a crane's bill, bristled seeds are actively ejected when mature.

Roots: Woody.

Culture

Exposure: Full sun to partial shade.
Soil: Loam to gravelly scree soils.
Soil Moisture: Moderate watering to dry.
Hardiness: USDA zones 4 to 8.
Elevation Range: Up to 7,500 feet.

Best Features

Like other geraniums, the foliage takes on lovely scarlet and purple tints and maintains color into early winter, but in LA VETA LACE geranium, the color lasts longer and is more intense than most. Finely dissected foliage and large flowers are very unusual for this genus.

Tucked in among other vegetation, LA VETA LACE geranium displays a throng of vivid purple-lilac blossoms.

Miscellaneous

This plant is tricky to propagate. Seeds are one option: cover them lightly, as light is not needed for germination. Cuttings are another option, but they need to be taken while the stems are still pink to reddish.

Glandularia bipinnatifida (Nutt.) Nutt.

VALLEY LAVENDER **plains verbena**

Pronunciation: **gland-you-LAIR-ee-ah by-pin-nah-TIFF-ih-dah**

Family: **Verbenaceae – verbena family**

Type of Plant: **Herbaceous perennial**

Height: **3 to 6 inches**

Spread: **12 to 18 inches**

Published: *Transactions of the American Philosophical Society, new series*, **5: 184. 1837.** (for the species)

Year Recommended: **2005**

Why Chosen

Verbenas are usually thought of as the brilliant red, pink, purple, or white annuals. Native-plant enthusiasts know of several verbenas from the Rocky Mountain region that are perennials and extremely drought tolerant. Several local nurseries have grown this plant as *Verbena bipinnatifida* for years. Little Valley Wholesale Nursery (Brighton, Colorado) developed a fine strain, which was then marketed as VALLEY LAVENDER plains verbena. It forms low, compact mats of gray foliage covered with rounded, dense spikes of bright lavender-purple flowers beginning in May. The plants bloom sporadically through summer, with a second generous flush of flowers in late summer and autumn. *Glandularia* is diminutive for the Latin *glandula*, a reference to the glandular mass found on the stigma lobes.

VALLEY LAVENDER plains verbena flowers are prominent in late spring and again early fall, with a sprinkling of flowers throughout the summer.

Landscape Use

A small-scale groundcover, VALLEY LAVENDER plains verbena looks equally at home in a formal garden or the wild garden; it is perfect for path edges, the front of the xeriscape, or in sunny perennial gardens, among rocks, and cascading over low walls.

Form

Prostrate ground-hugging mat with loosely ascending stems.

Native Range of Species

Great Plains of North America, southwest to Arizona and into Mesoamerica to Nicaragua; in plains, prairies, meadows, roadsides, along streams, and in disturbed sites; 250 to 7,500 feet.

Characteristics

Flowers: Tubular with spreading petals, to about ⅔ inch long and ¾ inch wide, borne in short compressed spikes, nectariferous, bright lavender-purple, May to October.
Leaves: Opposite, bipinnately compound, 1 to 2½ inches long, covered with coarse hairs above and beneath, edges often rolled under, gray-green.
Stems: Prostrate to ascending, densely covered with stiff, coarse hairs.
Fruits: Four nutlets.

Culture

Exposure: Full sun.
Soil: Garden loam, clay, or sandy soil.
Soil Moisture: Moderate watering to xeric.
Hardiness: USDA zones 4 to 8.
Elevation Range: Up to 6,000 feet.

Best Features

Once established, it requires only occasional watering to encourage lavish flowering. The flowering season can extend well into the winter in mild years.

Disadvantages

Intolerant of too much shade or excessive watering.

Miscellaneous

VALLEY LAVENDER plains verbena was selected from a local genotype for cold hardiness and flower color. Plants must be produced from stem cuttings, which root easily.

Native Americans rubbed crushed leaves on snakebites and used an infusion made from leaves as a gargle to treat sore throats.

Previously listed as *Verbena bipinnatifida* Schauer by Plant Select.

Heuchera sanguinea Engelm. 'Snow Angel'
Snow Angel coral bells

The panicles peek through the leaves of Snow Angel coral bells, adding a splash of color to a garden's early season.

Pronunciation: **HEW-ker-ah san-GWIN-ee-ah**

Family: **Saxifragaceae – saxifrage family**

Type of Plant: **Herbaceous perennial**

Height: **12 to 15 inches**

Spread: **8 to 12 inches**

Published: ***Memoir of a Tour to Northern Mexico*** **107. 1848. (for the species, not the cultivar)**

Year Recommended: **2003**

Why Chosen

Harlan Hamernik selected this unusual variegated form of the Southwest native species from a seedling population growing at Bluebird Nursery (Clarkson, Nebraska). The low-growing mounds of light green, broadly lobed leaves are marbled with a light cream variegation that will brighten any shady garden. Long-lasting panicles of bright pink-red bells appear on sturdy stems and float above the distinctive mound of foliage from late spring into summer. Remove faded flower stems to encourage formation of additional panicles. The species' name describes the blood red to carmine color of the flowers. This plant is adapted to monsoonal climates that have inconsistent wet seasons.

Though the flowers are typical of *Heuchera sanguinea*, the leaves of this cultivar make it out-of-the-ordinary, especially in early morning or evening light.

Landscape Use

Attractive as an accent plant, in massing or in drifts; an excellent plant for dry shade areas of the garden or the front to center of the border.

Form

Low, compact mounding perennial.

Native Range of Species

New Mexico to Arizona, into northern Mexico; in moist, shady rocky areas in mountains; 4,000 to 8,500 feet.

Characteristics

Flowers: Campanulate, less than ⅛ inch long, bright pink-red, on racemose panicles, late spring into summer.

Leaves: Alternate, blades palmately lobed, circular to ovate, to 2½ inches across, green marbled with light cream variegation, glandular-puberulent.

Stems: Scapose, to 15 inches, bases sheathed in persistent petioles.

Fruits: Capsules to about 3/16 inch long.

Culture

Exposure: Partial sun to shade.

Soil: Average garden loam to gravelly soil.

Soil Moisture: Moderate watering.

Hardiness: USDA zones 3 to 9.

Elevation Range: Up to 8,000 feet.

Best Features

Performs well in dry shade. Variegated foliage.

Disadvantages

Availability has been limited, but more nationwide growers are now producing this spectacular plant.

Miscellaneous

Plants are produced from stem cuttings to maintain consistent variegation.

Heuchera sanguinea 'Snow Angel' 135

Oenothera macrocarpa Nutt. subsp. *incana* (A. Gray) W. L. Wagner

SILVER BLADE evening primrose

Silvery leaves with a slight sheen enhance SILVER BLADE evening primrose's significant flowers, creating a breathtaking blend of color and texture.

Pronunciation: **ee-noh-THEER-ah mack-row-CAR-pah subspecies in-KANE-nah**

Family: **Onagraceae – evening primrose family**

Type of Plant: **Herbaceous perennial**

Height: **4 to 6 inches**

Spread: **12 to 15 inches**

Published: *Annals of the Missouri Botanical Garden* **70(1): 194. 1983.**

Year Introduced: **1999**

Why Chosen

Few classic garden plants bloom as prolifically or for as long as this evening primrose. The waxy silver leaves are stunning in their own right, but provide a perfect foil for the immense lemon yellow flowers. This selection was brought to Plant Select by Harlan Hamernik of Bluebird Nursery (Clarkson, Nebraska), who collected it with staff from the Dyck Arboretum of the Plains (Hesston, Kansas) and the Nebraska Statewide Arboretum (Lincoln, Nebraska). The species' name means large (*macro*) fruit (*carpa*), which, in addition, bear pronounced, attractive ridges, or wings.

Silver sage merges beautifully with SILVER BLADE evening primrose.

Landscape Use

Ideal for xeriscapes and prairie gardens, as the forefront of the traditional perennial border, along pathways, in rock gardens, and in shortgrass meadows.

Form

Erect, reclining with ascending tips or spreading stems form a low-mounding loose mat or groundcover.

Native Range of Species

This silver-leaved subspecies comes from the very southern and western extremity of the species' overall range, from southwest Kansas and western Oklahoma into the Texas Panhandle and possibly northeastern New Mexico; on limestone escarpments and dry prairie hills.

Characteristics

Flowers: Four-petaled, lemon yellow, often becoming reddish with age, to 4 inches across, floral tube 2 to 6 inches long, May to frost.

Leaves: Alternate, broadly elliptic to lanceolate, 1 to 4 inches long, entire, with pronounced silvery appressed, straight hairs or whitish short, soft hairs on both surfaces.

Stems: Semi-woody, reddish, erect to reclining with ascending tips, to 10 inches long.

Fruits: Capsules with wings to 1 inch wide on each of the four carpels, 2 to 3 inches long.

Roots: Substantial, fleshy perennial taproot.

Culture

Exposure: Full sun.

Soil: Average garden soil.

Soil Moisture: Moderate watering to dry.

Hardiness: USDA zones 4a to 9.

Elevation Range: Up to 8,000 feet.

Best Features

Large lemon yellow flowers. Large winged fruits. Reddish stems that contrast with the silvery foliage. This selection is even more drought tolerant than the typical green form of the species.

Disadvantages

Susceptible to flea beetles.

Miscellaneous

Plants grown from stem cuttings come true to the subspecies. If grown from seeds, you will need to rogue out the small percentage of green seedlings.

Pronunciation: **or-EGG-ah-num lee-bah-NOT-ih-cum**

Family: **Lamiaceae – mint family**

Type of Plant: **Herbaceous perennial**

Height: **10 to 15 inches**

Spread: **18 to 24 inches**

Published: ***Diagnoses Plantarum Orientalium Novarum, ser. 1,* 1(5): 14. 1844.**

Year Recommended: **2004**

B. Coogan

Why Chosen

The foliage of hopflower oregano is quite fine in texture and a subtle bluish gray-green color. However, its main attraction comes from the interesting hoplike inflorescences that dangle in abundance from thin, wiry stems. Delicate pinkish lavender flowers emerge from between the chartreuse-toned bracts beginning in early summer and continuing for many weeks. After flowering ceases, the flower stems become dry and turn tan. Seeds of this species were originally obtained by Denver Botanic Gardens from Carman's Nursery in Los Gatos, California, which obtained seeds from J. H. Ietswaart, monographer of the genus. The species' name pays homage to its homeland, Lebanon.

Midsummer brings out hopflower oregano's inimitable flowers, which are produced until fall. This fairly large, noticeable individual can stand on its own or work as an accent plant.

Landscape Use

Best used as an accent plant and in small groupings in planters, containers, and rock gardens. Situate where it can drape or trail over stones or low walls to best show the display of interesting flowers.

Form

Low-mounding, trailing, sprawling, draping, densely branched perennial.

Native Range

This species is endemic in the northern Lebanon Mountains; in dry regions; 2,300 to 6,550 feet.

Characteristics

Flowers: Two-lipped, to ½ inch long, pinkish lavender, borne on a spike of densely overlapping chartreuse bracts, summer to fall.
Leaves: Opposite, rounded to ovate, to ½ inch long and ⅓ inch wide, light bluish gray-green, nearly hairless.
Stems: Yellowish or purplish brown, to 15 inches.
Fruits: Four nutlets.

Culture

Exposure: Full sun to partial shade.
Soil: Well-drained garden loam, clay, or sandy soil.
Soil Moisture: Moderate watering.
Hardiness: USDA zones 4b to 8.
Elevation Range: Up to 7,000 feet.

Best Features

Long flowering season. Excellent plant to drape or sprawl over walls or rocks. Eye-pleasing bluish gray-green foliage. Dried flower stems are ideal for floral arrangements, or if left on the plant, they add a charming rustle in late summer and autumn breezes.

Miscellaneous

Plants will root easily from vegetative growth. Once the plants begin to flower, forget about propagating from stem cuttings.

Osteospermum barberiae (Harv.) Norl. var. compactum Milford
PURPLE MOUNTAIN sun daisy

Classic daisy flowers fill a flower bed with enjoyment during the first half of the growing season.

Pronunciation: **oss-tee-oh-SPER-mum bar-BER-ee-eye variety com-PACT-um**

Family: **Asteraceae – sunflower family**

Type of Plant: **Herbaceous perennial**

Height: **8 to 12 inches**

Spread: **10 to 15 inches**

Published: *Studien Calendar i.* 257. 1943. (for the species, not the variety)

Year Introduced: **1998**

Margaret Sjoelin

Why Chosen

Of the many sorts of African daisies, the osteospermums are perhaps the most widely used, especially the famous "freeway daisies" of California roadsides. Plant Select was the first to introduce this brilliant violet-red hardy African daisy native from the highest elevations of the Drakensberg Mountains. The dense mats of oblong leaves are evergreen and aromatic if brushed. These mats are obscured by the bright flowers through spring, with intermittent floral coverage until autumn frosts. The species' name commemorates Mrs. F. W. Barber, from whom botanist William H. Harvey received seeds and dried specimens.

Although PURPLE MOUNTAIN sun daisy grows well in bright, sunny locations, moderate to moist well-drained soil is essential for plant vigor.

Landscape Use

Lovely as an accent plant, in massing or in drifts, in the foreground of mixed or perennial borders, in planters, or in containers.

Form

Low-mounding, compact variety of the species, often forms dense mats.

Native Range of Species

Summits of the Drakensberg Mountains, Eastern Cape and Natal provinces, South Africa.

Characteristics

Flowers: Daisylike heads to 2½ inches across, borne singly on stalks to 3 inches long, ray flowers are brilliant violet-red, disk flowers purple, April to spring and intermittently until frost.
Leaves: Alternate, linear-oblong to spatulate, 2 to 3 inches long, entire to finely toothed, rich green, aromatic.
Stems: Woody at base, producing an abundance of herbaceous shoots perennially, erect, sparsely covered with short, soft hairs.
Fruits: Achenes.

Culture

Exposure: Full sun to partial shade.
Soil: Ordinary garden loam.
Soil Moisture: Moist to moderate watering.
Hardiness: USDA zones 4b to 9.
Elevation Range: Up to 7,000 feet.

Best Features

Compact habit. Brilliant violet-red flowers.

Disadvantages

Persistent winter moisture may cause plants to rot.

Miscellaneous

Plants are easily rooted from stem cuttings, however they are extremely susceptible to fungal pathogens. Remove flower buds to encourage rooting.

Osteospermum L. sp.
Lavender Mist sun daisy

As their names imply, both Lavender Mist and Purple Mountain sun daisies' ray flowers open only during sunlight hours.

Pronunciation: **oss-tee-oh-SPER-mum species**

Family: **Asteraceae – sunflower family**

Type of Plant: **Herbaceous perennial**

Height: **10 to 12 inches**

Spread: **12 to 15 inches**

Year Introduced: **1998**

Why Chosen

This vigorous mat-forming daisy from South Africa is even more robust than Purple Mountain sun daisy, which was introduced the same year. The flowers can be 3 inches across and are produced in flushes throughout the entire growing season. They open a pure glistening white and age to a blush lavender color, for which the plant is named. Plants covered with both flower color tones are exceptionally striking. This selection appears to be of hybrid origin because it is much more vigorous than other high mountain African daisies. Original germplasm was gifted to Denver Botanic Gardens from Blooming Nursery (Cornelius, Oregon).

White flowers gradually transform to soft lavender.

Landscape Use

Attractive as an accent plant, in massing and drifts, in the foreground of mixed or perennial borders, and in planters or containers.

Form

Low-mounding, compact variety of the species, often forms dense mats.

Native Range of Species

Purported to be a naturally occurring hybrid, parents and nativity are unknown.

Characteristics

Flowers: Daisylike heads to 3 inches across, solitary on short stalks, ray flowers are white changing to soft lavender, disk flowers are deep purple, April to fall.
Leaves: Alternate, linear-oblong to spatulate, 2 to 3 inches long, mostly entire, nearly succulent, evergreen.
Stems: Woody at base, herbaceous above, erect to trailing, sparsely covered with short, soft hairs, nearly succulent.
Fruits: Achenes.

Culture

Exposure: Full sun to partial shade.
Soil: Garden loam.
Soil Moisture: Moderate watering.
Hardiness: USDA zones 4b to 8.
Elevation Range: Up to 7,000 feet.

Best Features

Long flowering season. Ray flowers change from white to soft lavender.

Miscellaneous

Plants are easily rooted from stem cuttings; however, they are extremely susceptible to fungal pathogens. Remove flower buds to encourage rooting.

Osteospermum sp. 143

Penstemon linarioides A. Gray subsp. *coloradoensis* (A. Nelson) D. D. Keck
Silverton bluemat penstemon

Silverton bluemat penstemon is petite and can be tucked between and around rocks in a rock garden.

Pronunciation: PEN-steh-mon lin-air-ee-OY-dees
          subspecies col-uh-rod-oh-EN-sis

Family: **Scrophulariaceae – figwort family**

Type of Plant: **Herbaceous perennial**

Height: **8 to 12 inches**

Spread: **12 to 15 inches**

Published: ***Bulletin of the Torrey Botanical Club*** 64(6): 375. 1937.

Year Recommended: **2005**

Why Chosen

This penstemon subspecies has stunning silvery blue-green foliage that distinguishes it from the typical species. Its growth habit is compact, forming a low mound 8 inches tall and 12 to 15 inches wide. The nearly 1-inch-long pale, lavender-blue flowers are borne on short 4- to 6-inch spikes in May and June, increasing the height of the plant to about 12 inches. Additionally, this selection is extremely heat and drought tolerant. The foliage is evergreen and remains attractive into November. Its growth habit is reminiscent of *Penstemon pinifolius*. Panayoti Kelaidis collected seeds of this selection for Denver Botanic Gardens near Durango, Colorado.

This plant is well suited to a xeriscape setting.

Landscape Use

Suitable for mass plantings, drifts, raised beds, the front of mixed perennial borders, in rock gardens or naturalistic gardens.

Form

Low-mounding perennial.

Native Range of Subspecies

Southwest Colorado to northwest New Mexico; on dry, sandy, or rocky slopes in sagebrush, chaparral, or woodlands; 6,200 to 8,500 feet.

Characteristics

Flowers: Tubular, inflated, secund, to ⅔ inch long, lavender-blue, May and June.
Leaves: Opposite, linear to linear-lanceolate, to 1 inch long, covered with light gray, minute, soft straight hairs to hairless, silvery blue-green, evergreen.
Stems: Erect, simple or branched from stout woody caudex, numerous, covered with minute, soft straight hairs.
Fruits: Capsules.

Culture

Exposure: Full sun to partial shade.
Soil: Well-drained loam or sandy soil.
Soil Moisture: Moderate watering to xeric.
Hardiness: USDA zones 4 to 10.
Elevation Range: Up to 8,000 feet.

Best Features

Pale lavender-blue flowers beautifully accent the silvery blue-green foliage. Very drought tolerant. Short growth habit.

Miscellaneous

This subspecies should be propagated from cuttings to produce uniform plants. Stick multiple cuttings per pot to get fuller plants more quickly.

Previously listed as a variety by Plant Select, not as a subspecies.

Penstemon linarioides subsp. *coloradoensis* 145

Phlox bifida L. C. Beck
SNOWMASS phlox

SNOWMASS phlox, with its snowflake-shaped flowers, will carry the impression of winter into late spring and early summer.

Pronunciation: **flox BIFF-ih-dah**

Family: **Polemoniaceae – phlox family**

Type of Plant: **Herbaceous perennial**

Height: **4 to 8 inches**

Spread: **18 to 24 inches**

Published: *American Journal of Science, and Arts* **11(1): 170. 1826.**

Year Introduced: **2006**

Why Chosen

Phlox bifida is commonly called sand phlox because of its habitat and cleft phlox due to the unique shape of its petals. Each of the flower's five narrow petals is deeply cleft from the tip to one-half its length, giving the impression of a perfect snowflake. The plant forms a dense mat of evergreen foliage covered with glistening snowflake-shaped flowers for a month or more in early spring. Flower color of the typical species ranges from pale lavender to rose-lavender to deep lilac; SNOWMASS phlox is pure white, the least common flower color variant. This slow-growing phlox performs best if given good drainage and some shade.

Left: SNOWMASS phlox must be watered sparingly for the plant to thrive; adjust your lawn-watering zones accordingly.

Right: Tulips and SNOWMASS phlox will flower concurrently in April.

Landscape Use

Excellent for woodlands, shortgrass meadows, rock gardens, the front of the perennial border, and among rocks.

Form

Erect to reclining with tips ascending and sprawling stems form a low mound.

Native Range of Species

Southwest Michigan to Tennessee, west to Kansas and Arkansas; restricted to dry, sandy, or limestone soils, rocky grasslands, or upland woods; rare.

Characteristics

Flowers: Corolla tube five-lobed, each deeply cleft, nearly 1 inch across, white, flower stems covered with minute, soft, straight glandular hairs, April to June.
Leaves: Opposite, linear to lanceolate, stiff, 1 to 2 inches long, sharply pointed, dark green, nearly succulent, evergreen.
Stems: Erect to reclining with ascending tips.
Fruits: Capsules, three-valved.

Culture

Exposure: Full sun to partial shade.
Soil: Garden loam, clay, or sandy soil; needs good drainage.
Soil Moisture: Moderate watering to dry.
Hardiness: USDA zones 4b to 9.
Elevation Range: Up to 7,000 feet.

Best Features

Dark green, evergreen, nearly succulent foliage and snowflakelike flowers. Tolerates well-drained sandy, granitic, or alkaline soils.

Disadvantages

Limited commercial availability. Languishes in wet, poorly drained soils. Short-lived if overwatered.

Miscellaneous

Propagation is best done from stem cuttings taken from garden-grown stock. Stems can be layered in the garden, but rooting percentages are low.

Plants from granite areas of the southeastern Ozarks usually bear the deeper lilac to rose-lavender shades; plants from the sandy prairies or other prairie areas in northern Illinois often produce predominantly white flowers.

Salvia daghestanica Sosn.
PLATINUM sage

PLATINUM sage's dark blue flowers bloom in profusion in May and June.

Pronunciation: **SAL-vee-ah DAG-eh-STAN-ih-kah**

Family: **Lamiaceae – mint family**

Type of Plant: **Herbaceous perennial**

Height: **8 to 10 inches**

Spread: **12 to 18 inches**

Published: ***Notizen Systematik Geographica Institut Botanica Thbiliss* Fasc. 16: 9. 1951.**

Year Recommended: **2006**

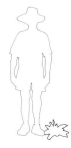

Why Chosen

The dark blue flowers of PLATINUM sage contrast with an electric intensity against silver foliage that is indeed stunning. Like silver sage and cashmere sage, the flowers are borne in orderly whorls, creating a wonderful architectural component to the landscape. The neat silver rosettes of foliage are perfect for edging sunny, dry borders or can easily be tucked into the rock garden in tidy clumps. PLATINUM sage's compact size makes it extremely versatile in the landscape. As flowering diminishes, the rosettes of textured, silvery leaves continue to draw attention into the weeks of winter. Think of this plant as a reliably perennial dusty miller.

For most of the growing season, the basal leaves provide a rich silvery groundcover.

Landscape Use

Ideal as an accent plant or in small groups, for the sunny, dry garden, in the front of a perennial border, or among rocks.

Form

Low-mounding rosettes of leaves covered densely with silvery, woolly hairs.

Native Range of Species

Endemic in the North Caucasus Mountains of Daghestan in southernmost Russia; on dry, stony slopes and in middle and upper mountain zones.

Characteristics

Flowers: Tubular, two-lipped, upper lip somewhat dorsally concave, to ⅔ inch long, dark blue, borne in five- to six-flowered verticillasters, three to six spaced verticillasters per stem, spring and early summer.

Leaves: Opposite, oblong-spatulate, subentire with obtuse teeth toward tip, up to 4 inches long, covered densely with silvery, woolly hairs above and beneath, year-round appeal.

Stems: From a woody branching rhizome, flower stems erect, simple, covered densely with woolly hairs near base, with fine glandular hairs above.

Fruits: Four nutlets.

Culture

Exposure: Full sun to partial shade.

Soil: Garden loam or sandy soil, well drained.

Soil Moisture: Moderate watering to xeric; good drainage.

Hardiness: USDA zones 5 to 10.

Elevation Range: Up to 6,000 feet.

Best Features

Dark blue flowers. Silvery, woolly leaves. Clumping growth habit. Tolerates dry, poor soils.

Disadvantages

Does not perform well in poorly drained soils.

Miscellaneous

Plants can be grown from cuttings or seeds. Seeds germinate readily but require light. Cuttings root easily but can take a long time for adequate root development.

PLATINUM sage has proven resistant to browsing by deer and rabbits.

Satureja montana L. subsp. *illyrica* Nyman
Purple winter savory

Purple winter savory is swathed in tiny flowers from late summer through fall.

Pronunciation: **sa-TOUR-ee-ah mon-TAN-ah subspecies il-LEAR-ih-cah**

Family: **Lamiaceae – mint family**

Type of Plant: **Herbaceous perennial**

Height: **4 to 6 inches**

Spread: **12 to 15 inches**

Published: *Florae Europaea* 3: 164. 1972.

Year Recommended: **2007**

Why Chosen

Purple winter savory begins to leaf out in March and can even produce early but somewhat sporadic flowers. Its dark green glossy foliage is persistent into the early weeks of winter and can remain evergreen if planted in a protected microclimate. The Plant Select selection has flowers that are deep violet-lavender. They are borne in few-flowered whorls that are congested at the tips of the flower stems, engulfing the plant in a soft glow that is strikingly beautiful and often unexpected. The main flowering period begins in August and continues as late as mid-November, when many garden perennials look bedraggled from the long hot summer.

One of the most durable plants for the garden, purple winter savory's dark green leaves give beds valued color throughout most of the year.

Landscape Use

The compact size of purple winter savory is perfect for planting at the front of the border, in containers, or the mixed border.

Form

Makes a very short and compact mounding subshrub.

Native Range of Subspecies

This subspecies is found along the east coastal region of the Adriatic Sea from Trieste south to northern Albania; usually found growing on rocky slopes.

Characteristics

Flowers: Tubular, four-lobed, two-lipped, to about ½ inch long, deep violet-lavender, borne in dense, closely spaced verticillasters, nectariferous, August to October.
Leaves: Opposite, linear-lanceolate, to about 1 inch long, slighty rough to the touch, covered with minute, soft straight hairs, glossy, leathery, dark green, situationally evergreen.
Stems: Woody at base with herbaceous new shoots, erect to reclining with tips ascending, without hairs.
Fruits: Four nutlets.

Culture

Exposure: Full sun to partial shade.
Soil: Garden loam, clay, or sandy soil that is well drained.
Soil Moisture: Moderate watering to xeric, once established.
Hardiness: USDA zones 3b to 8.
Elevation Range: Up to 9,000 feet.

Best Features

Grows well in a variety of different exposures, soil types, and moistures. Compact habit.

Disadvantages

Tends to go dormant and die back to the ground from mid-December through February.

Miscellaneous

These plants are easily grown from seeds; do not cover the seeds as they need light to germinate.

Very attractive to sphinx moths, which visit for nectar late in the afternoon.

Purple winter savory can be used as a culinary herb, but this subspecies tends to be a little more acrid than the species.

Previously listed as a variety by Plant Select, not as a subspecies.

Scutellaria suffrutescens S. Watson
Cherry skullcap

Bristling with cherry red flowers shaped like skullcaps, this tiny plant can put on quite a show all by itself.

Pronunciation: SCOO-tel-lar-ee-ah suf-FRU-tess-ens

Family: **Lamiaceae – mint family**

Type of Plant: **Tender perennial**

Height: **3 to 8 inches**

Spread: **10 to 15 inches**

Published: *Proceedings of the American Academy of Arts and Sciences* 25: 160. 1890. (for the species, not this selection)

Year Recommended: **2004**

Claudia Anderson
09

Why Chosen

Cherry skullcap is named for its distinctive tubular, cherry red, helmetlike "skullcap" flowers, which are produced in profusion from summer to fall. This selection differs from the wild species, which has yellow flowers with red markings. Its numerous stems form a dense, low-mounding plant that is somewhat woody at the base. The small, slightly hairy ovate leaves are distinctively nerved beneath. Occasional light shearing will encourage an even greater number of buds and blooms. John Fairey and Carl Schoenfeld (Yucca Do Nursery, Hempstead, Texas) collected the original germplasm of this species in gypsum barrens near Galeana, Nuevo León, Mexico, and Bluebird Nursery (Clarkson, Nebraska) provided plants to Plant Select.

Backlighting enhances the appearance of any flower; cherry skullcap is no exception.

Landscape Use

Cherry skullcap will brighten the front of the border in a bed of perennials or in rock gardens. It also works well as a hardy annual at higher elevations.

Form

Naturally compact and low mounding.

Native Range of Species

In the states of Coahuila, Nuevo León, and Tamaulipas, Mexico; 2,300 to 10,200 feet.

Characteristics

Flowers: Tubular, two-lipped, to about ⅘ inch long, axillary, cherry red, in axils of upper leaves, summer to fall.
Leaves: Opposite, sessile, ovate to oblong-ovate, to ½ inch long, entire, strongly nerved beneath, covered with short, soft, silvery hairs.
Stems: Woody at the base, producing an abundance of new shoots each year, rigid, multibranched, covered with minute, soft straight hairs.
Fruits: Four nutlets.

Culture

Exposure: Full sun to partial shade.
Soil: Garden loam or sandy soil.
Soil Moisture: Moderate watering to dry.
Hardiness: USDA zones 6 to 9 (possible perennial in protected sites in zone 5a).
Elevation Range: Up to 5,400 feet.

Best Features

Long flowering season. Requires water to establish but minimal thereafter. Flowers are produced abundantly.

Disadvantages

Intolerant of poorly drained soils and wet situations.

Miscellaneous

This plant is propagated from cuttings, but because they flower prolifically, finding good vegetative growth can be challenging.

Cherry skullcap is reported to be deer resistant.

Veronica liwanensis K. Koch
Turkish veronica

Turkish veronica, snow-in-summer, and rock soapwort create a luxuriant melding of colors for late spring gardens.

Pronunciation: **Ver-ON-ih-cah LEE-wan-en-sis**

Family: **Scrophulariaceae – figwort family**

Type of Plant: **Herbaceous perennial**

Height: **1 to 2 inches**

Spread: **15 to 18 inches**

Published: *Linnaea* 22: 698. 1849.

Year Introduced: **1997**

Why Chosen

This evergreen groundcover was introduced by the University of British Columbia expedition to northwestern Turkey led by Roy Davidson, James MacPhail, and John Watson in 1977. For virtually all of April and May, the mats are obscured under a mass of brilliant cobalt blue, four-petaled flowers. The mat grows thickly enough to discourage most weeds but makes a perfect foil to and groundcover over bulbs. This vigorous groundcover seems to thrive in almost any soil or watering regime except bog or deep shade. The species' name refers to a geographic area in Turkey called Liwaneh (a Pashto word meaning "crazy"), where it was collected. This has been the most popular Plant Select introduction based on number of plants sold.

Characteristics

Flowers: Tubular with four spreading petals to ½ inch across, borne in many-flowered axillary racemes, cobalt blue, April to June.

Leaves: Opposite, lanceolate to ovate, 3/16 to 3/8 inch long, margins shallowly round-toothed, slightly covered with a bloom that can be rubbed off, mostly without hairs, leathery, dark green with purplish tints in winter, evergreen.

Stems: Woody at the base, prostrate or creeping with ascending tips, covered densely with short, soft hairs.

Fruits: Capsules, subelliptic to obcordate, to 3/8 inch long, covered with short, soft hairs.

Culture

Exposure: Full sun to partial shade.

Soil: Loam, clay, or sand; needs light fertilizing in sandy soil.

Soil Moisture: Average to completely dry, once established.

Hardiness: USDA zones 3 to 10.

Elevation Range: Up to 10,000 feet.

Best Features

Very tolerant of drought and alkaline soil.

Disadvantages

Intolerant of wet situations. Tolerates only light foot traffic.

Landscape Use

Great as a groundcover along path edges and among rocks, excellent cover over minor bulbs and in crevices of paving stones.

Form

Prostrate mat-forming plant.

Native Range of Species

Pontic Mountains in northeastern Turkey; among limestone and igneous rocks, on ledges, in crevices and scree, in alpine pastures and spruce forests; 980 to 7,860 feet.

Miscellaneous

These plants are propagated from stem cuttings, which root readily at almost any time of the year. Place several cuttings per pot to make a larger plant more quickly.

Veronica L. 'Reavis'

CRYSTAL RIVER veronica

Pronunciation: **Ver-ON-ih-cah**

Family: **Scrophulariaceae – figwort family**

Type of Plant: **Herbaceous perennial**

Height: **2 to 3 inches**

Spread: **20 to 30 inches**

Year Introduced: **2003**

Why Chosen

This fast-spreading groundcover, a spontaneous hybrid between *Veronica liwanensis* and *V. pectinata*, was found at Denver Botanic Gardens in 1998. Its foliage is intermediate between the parents: hairy and slightly lobed like the latter, and almost as compact as the former. This hybrid displays tremendous vigor, growing almost twice as quickly as either parent. *Veronica* 'Reavis' shows even wider climatic tolerance than *V. liwanensis* and tolerates relatively dense shade with equanimity. CRYSTAL RIVER veronica commemorates a tumbling watercourse in the West Elk Mountains that flows into the Roaring Fork River near Glenwood Springs, Colorado. The cultivar is named for Diana Reavis, active member of Plant Select who was instrumental in propagating this hybrid while working at Gulley Greenhouse Inc. (Fort Collins, Colorado).

CRYSTAL RIVER veronica spreads readily and is tolerant of a wide range of growing conditions. When planted en masse, mounds of CRYSTAL RIVER veronica's light blue flowers give the impression of a blue river.

Landscape Use

Great groundcover along path edges and among rocks, excellent cover over minor bulbs, in crevices of paving stones.

Form

Prostrate mat-forming plant.

Native Range of Species

Natural hybrid found at Denver Botanic Gardens. Both parents are native to Turkey—*Veronica liwanensis* in the northeast and *V. pectinata* occurs in the central and western part of the country in *Quercus* and *Pinus* forest, olive groves, steppes, dry, rocky places, fields, roadsides; 80 to 5,240 feet.

Characteristics

Flowers: Tubular with four spreading petals to ½ inch across, borne in many-flowered axillary racemes, pale blue with white throat, April to June and scattered thereafter.

Leaves: Opposite, lanceolate to ovate, ⅜ inch long, margins saw-toothed to shallowly round-toothed, slightly covered with a bloom that can be rubbed off, covered with coarse hairs, leathery, dark green with purplish tints in winter, evergreen.

Stems: Somewhat woody at the base, prostrate or creeping with ascending tips, covered densely with short, soft hairs.

Fruits: Capsules, obcordate to ¼ inch long, without hairs.

Culture

Exposure: Full sun to partial shade.
Soil: Clay, loam, or sandy soil.
Soil Moisture: Moderate watering to dry.
Hardiness: USDA zones 3 to 9.
Elevation Range: Up to 8,000 feet.

Best Features

Very tolerant of drought and alkaline soil.

Disadvantages

Intolerant of wet situations, but more tolerant than *Veronica liwanensis*. Tolerates only light foot traffic.

Miscellaneous

These plants are propagated from stem cuttings, which root readily at almost any time of the year. Place several cuttings per pot to make a larger plant more quickly.

Previously listed as *Veronica* L. ×'Reavis' by Plant Select.

Corsican violet

Pronunciation: **vee-OH-lah COR-sih-kah**

Family: **Violaceae – violet family**

Type of Plant: **Herbaceous perennial**

Height: **6 to 8 inches**

Spread: **6 to 8 inches**

Published: *Sylloge Flora Europa* 228. 1854.

Year Recommended: **2003**

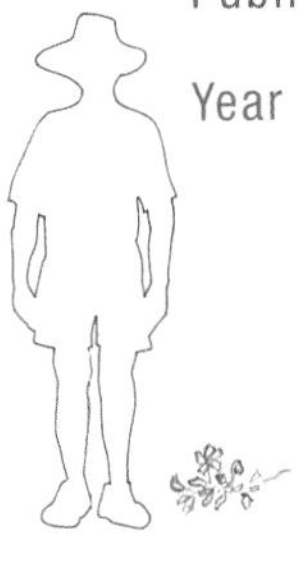

Linda Darcy

Why Chosen

Plants that adapt to diverse locations and growing conditions are worth their weight in gold to gardeners. Adaptability is all about succeeding and surviving when conditions are challenging, and the pretty little Corsican violet is noted for shrugging off the heat of summer and the chill of late autumn and early spring. Violets are cherished for their cheerful flowers, and this one sports vivid violet-blue faces with whiskerlike markings. The flowers appear in early spring, continue into the summer, and, without missing a beat, march on through the fall. Once planted in your garden, it may naturalize conservatively by self-seeding.

Violets are equated with being delicate and shrinking from adversity, but Corsican violets are just the opposite: they are very durable and tolerate a wide variety of climatic and soil conditions.

Landscape Use

Because of its small stature, Corsican violet is easy to use as a low-growing complement around shrubs, under trees, or in beds or borders as companions for other perennials, annuals, ornamental grasses, or spring flowering bulbs. Great in rock gardens.

Form

Low-mounding perennial.

Native Range of Species

Corsica, Sardinia, and Elba islands; among spiny shrubs and in rocky meadows; 1,950 to 5,890 feet.

Characteristics

Flowers: Five-petaled, borne singly on long stalk, ½ to 1⅓ inches across, petals barely overlapping, spur long, vivid violet-blue, early spring to late fall.

Leaves: Alternate, basal rhomboid-lanceolate, margins round-toothed, with basal linear-lobed stipules, upper leaves oblong to lanceolate, margins nearly entire.

Stems: Ascending, leafy, forming low mounds.

Fruits: Capsules to ½ inch long, many-seeded.

Culture

Exposure: Full sun to partial shade.
Soil: Rich loam to clay or gravelly soil.
Soil Moisture: Moderate watering.
Hardiness: USDA zones 3 to 8.
Elevation Range: Up to 9,000 feet.

Best Features

Vivid violet-blue flowers. Hardiness. Tolerance of sunny and shady exposures. Long flowering season. Spreads locally by self-seeding.

Miscellaneous

Most plants are grown from seeds. Their physiological dormancy requires a thirty-day cold stratification before sowing. Some success can be had from rooting stem cuttings.

Silver dollar plant with coleus.

Annuals

Clockwise from top: Ruby Moon hyacinth bean,
silver dollar plant, silver dollar plant.

Dolichos lablab L. 'Ruby Moon'
Ruby Moon hyacinth bean

Pronunciation: **DOLE-ee-khose LAB-lab**

Family: **Fabaceae – bean family**

Type of Plant: **Annual vine**

Height: **72 to 120 inches trellised**

Spread: **36 to 60 inches untrellised**

Published: ***Species Plantarum* 2: 725. 1753.**
           (for the species, not the cultivar)

Year Recommended: **2006**

Why Chosen

Ruby Moon hyacinth bean is a vigorous vining cousin to garden beans but with dark-purple-stained foliage, attractive in its own right. The generous clusters of deep amethyst-violet flowers resemble those of a delicate wisteria and are produced abundantly from midsummer to the frosty days of autumn. By August, expect this plant to be a focal point in your garden with hundreds of flowers produced together with huge, flat, dark violet glossy legumes contrasting with the purple leaves. The collective purple mass is absolutely stunning when backlit by waning sunlight during late afternoon and early evening hours.

The first season of interest for Ruby Moon hyacinth bean is late spring, when pealike flowers appear. In late summer, dark violet legumes adorn the plants.

Landscape Use

An essential addition to a wall, fence, arbor, or pergola. Creates graceful mounds in the annual or perennial border.

Form

Spreading, open, airy, upright branches forming a rounded or vaselike shape.

Native Range of Species

Old World, most likely tropical Africa.

Characteristics

Flowers: Pealike, about ½ inch long, several per 4- to 5-inch raceme, deep amethyst-violet, late spring to frost.
Leaves: Alternate, trifoliolate, leaflets nearly cordate, dark purplish green.
Stems: Thin, twining, nearly hairless.
Fruits: Legumes, to about 2 inches long, showy dark violet, late summer.

Culture

Exposure: Full sun to partial shade.
Soil: Average garden loam.
Soil Moisture: Moderate watering.
Hardiness: USDA zones 7 to 11, annual elsewhere.
Elevation Range: Up to 7,000 feet.

Best Features

Purple color from rapidly growing vine. Long season of appeal. Ideal for an instant seasonal screen.

Disadvantages

Susceptible to spider mites.

Miscellaneous

Hyacinth bean is easily grown from seeds. Soak them in hot water for an hour to help improve germination.

Hyacinth bean is a culinary staple in southern Asia and much of Africa; however, young pods, leaves, as well as the soft immature seeds can be toxic. All parts require several changes of water during preparation.

Used for erosion control, as a green manure, and as a fodder for cattle in Nigeria.

Melinis nerviglumis (Franch.) Zizka
PINK CRYSTALS ruby grass

The bluish gray-green leaves of PINK CRYSTALS ruby grass add fine texture to the garden throughout summer.

Pronunciation: **mel-EYE-niss ner-vih-GLOOM-iss**

Family: **Poaceae – grass family**

Type of Plant: **Annual ornamental grass**

Height: **20 to 24 inches**

Spread: **12 to 15 inches**

Published: *Bibliotheca Botanica* **138: 111. 1988.**

Year Introduced: **1998**

Why Chosen

PINK CRYSTALS ruby grass was first grown at Denver Botanic Gardens in the 1980s from seeds distributed by the Drakensberg Botanic Garden in Harrismith, South Africa (now Harrismith Wildflower Gardens). Although this astonishing grass is an annual in USDA hardiness zones 6 or colder, it is nonetheless a superb accent plant. It has such shimmering pink-and-silver panicled inflorescences in late summer that it is well worth including in any landscape design. Small plants should be set into the garden in late May, and by late August you can expect the flowering spectacle to begin, lasting until hard frost.

The pink-and-silver inflorescences change to tawny brown late in the growing season.

Landscape Use

Lovely as an accent plant, in mass plantings, drifts, the middle of mixed perennial or annual borders, planters, containers, and raised beds.

Form

Numerous stems arise from a small crown to form a densely tufted, very attractive clump.

Native Range of Species

Sub-Saharan Africa and Madagascar; in open grasslands and stony hillsides; 1,300 to 7,100 feet.

Characteristics

Flowers: Borne on a panicle of spikelets that are covered densely with silvery pink hairs, August to hard frost.
Leaves: Alternate, blades to 11 inches long, basal leaf sheaths strongly overlapping, pale bluish gray-green.
Stems: Stout, sturdy, resilient, not easily susceptible to lodging.

Culture

Exposure: Full sun to partial shade.
Soil: Ordinary loam is best.
Soil Moisture: Moderate watering.
Hardiness: USDA zones 4 to 6.
Elevation Range: Up to 8,000 feet.

Best Features

Unique pinkish inflorescences and pale bluish gray-green stems and leaves. Densely tufted habit.

Disadvantages

This species grows somewhat slowly; use the largest possible plants in your planting designs to garner the earliest possible flowering.

Miscellaneous

This grass is easily grown from seeds. Sow seeds in midwinter to achieve larger plants at transplanting time. A trick to producing larger plants is to group multiple seedlings together when transplanting from the seed pan.

Previously listed as *Rhynchelytrum nerviglume* (Franch.) Choiv. by Plant Select.

Plectranthus argentatus S.T. Blake
Silver dollar plant

The leaves of silver dollar plant add charm to planters, here mixed with coleus.

Pronunciation: **PLECK-tran-thus ar-gen-TAY-tus**

Family: **Lamiaceae – mint family**

Type of Plant: **Annual**

Height: **20 to 36 inches**

Spread: **20 to 40 inches**

Published: *Contributions from the Queensland Herbarium* **9: 27. 1971.**

Year Recommended: **1999**

Why Chosen

One of the few annuals recommended by Plant Select, this shrubby Australian mint is perennial where frost does not occur. This fast-growing plant is best started fresh each spring. The narrow stalks of bluish white flowers are not very showy but add interest late in the season. Original germplasm for this plant was acquired by Rick Darke at Titoki Point Garden and Nursery on the North Island of Australia and introduced through Longwood Gardens' (Kennett Square, Pennsylvania) plant introduction program. The species' name refers to the abundance of silvery recurved hairs on the leaves and young stems.

Early in the season, the leaves of silver dollar plant are its appealing feature, while the relatively insignificant flowers take a backseat.

Flowers become showier toward the end of summer.

Landscape Use

Excellent as an accent or massed, in containers, annual plantings, or borders.

Form

Densely branched, medium-sized mound.

Native Range of Species

North-central New South Wales and along border with Queensland, Australia; grows in rocky areas, frequently associated with waterfalls, uncommon; perennial in nature, becoming a subshrub.

Characteristics

Flowers: Tubular, two-lipped, to ⅖ inch long, bluish white, summer to frost.

Leaves: Opposite, blades ovate to broadly ovate, typically to 2 inches long (longer in nature), margins shallowly round-toothed, covered densely with woolly hairs above and beneath, silver-green, mildly aromatic.

Stems: Erect to spreading, many-branched, densely covered with silvery recurved hairs.

Fruits: Four nutlets.

Culture

Exposure: Full sun to partial shade.

Soil: Ordinary loam is best.

Soil Moisture: Average to moderately dry.

Hardiness: USDA zones 10b to 11, annual elsewhere.

Elevation Range: Up to 7,000 feet.

Best Features

Rapidly forms deep roots. Nearly succulent, silvery green foliage. Tolerates neglect and drought with flair. Very attractive in containers to the end of the growing season.

Disadvantages

Annual in regions with frost.

Miscellaneous

Plants are in the mint family and will root very easily. There are some seed strains available, but the Plant Select variety is grown from cuttings.

Spanish Gold broom.

Appendices

Clockwise from upper left: SHADOW MOUNTAIN penstemon, SUNSET foxglove, chocolate flower, fernbush, alpine willowherb.

Scientific Name / Name used in trade* / page numbers	SPRING			SUMMER			AUTUMN			WINTER		
	Apr	May	Jun	Jul	Aug	Sep	Oct	Nov	Dec	Jan	Feb	Mar
Acer tataricum 'GarAnn'[PP15,023] — Hot Wings Tatarian maple — pages 14–15	■			▨	▨							
Arctostaphylos ×coloradoensis — Mock bearberry manzanita — pages 16–17	■										■	
Arctostaphylos ×coloradoensis — Panchito manzanita — pages 18–19	■										■	
Buddleja alternifolia 'Argentea' — Silver fountain butterfly bush — pages 20–21			■									
Chamaebatiaria millefolium — Fernbush — pages 22–23				■	■							
Cytisus purgans — Spanish Gold broom — pages 24–25		■										
Daphne ×burkwoodii 'Carol Mackie' — Carol Mackie daphne — pages 26–27	■											

Flowering ■ and Fruiting ▨ Seasons

Flower Color & Season	Fruit/Foliage Color & Season	Height (in feet unless marked inches)	Water Requirements	Sun Requirements	Elevation (in feet)
Greenish to yellowish white; April	Brilliant red samara late July–September; dark green changing from yellow to orange-red in fall, deciduous	15–18	Moderate watering	Full sun to partial shade	Up to 7,000
White to pale pink; February–April	Red berry, September–October; **evergreen foliage****, often turning rich reddish purple in fall	10–15 inches	Xeric once established	Full sun to partial shade	Up to 9,000
White to pale pink; February–April	Red berry, September–October; **evergreen foliage**, often turning rich reddish purple in fall	10–15 inches	Moderate watering to xeric once established	Full sun to partial shade	Up to 9,000
Lavender-blue to violet or purple; late spring	Brown capsule; leaves gray-green, deciduous	12–15	Moderate watering	Full sun to partial shade	Up to 8,000
White; mid-June–August	Brown follicle; leaves silvery green, **semi-deciduous**	3–5	Moderate watering; xeric once established	Full sun to partial shade	Up to 7,000
Bright golden yellow; mid–late spring	Blackish legume; leaves silvery green, often early deciduous	4–6	Average watering, not too wet	Full sun to partial shade	Up to 8,000
White flushed pink; early–mid-spring	**Somewhat persistent cream-edged green foliage**	3–4	Moderate watering	Sun or partial shade	Up to 9,000

Trees, Shrubs, and Woody Vines (Based upon information for Colorado USDA zone 5)

Scientific Name / Name used in trade* / page numbers	Flowering and Fruiting Seasons
	SPRING: Apr, May, Jun · SUMMER: Jul, Aug, Sep · AUTUMN: Oct, Nov, Dec · WINTER: Jan, Feb, Mar
Ephedra equisetina Bluestem joint fir pages 28–29	
Fallugia paradoxa Apache plume pages 30–31	
Jamesia americana Waxflower pages 32–33	
Lonicera korolkowii 'Floribunda' BLUE VELVET honeysuckle pages 34–35	
Lonicera prolifera KINTZLEY'S GHOST honeysuckle pages 36–37	
Paxistima canbyi Mountain lover pages 38–39	
Philadelphus lewisii CHEYENNE mock orange pages 40–41	

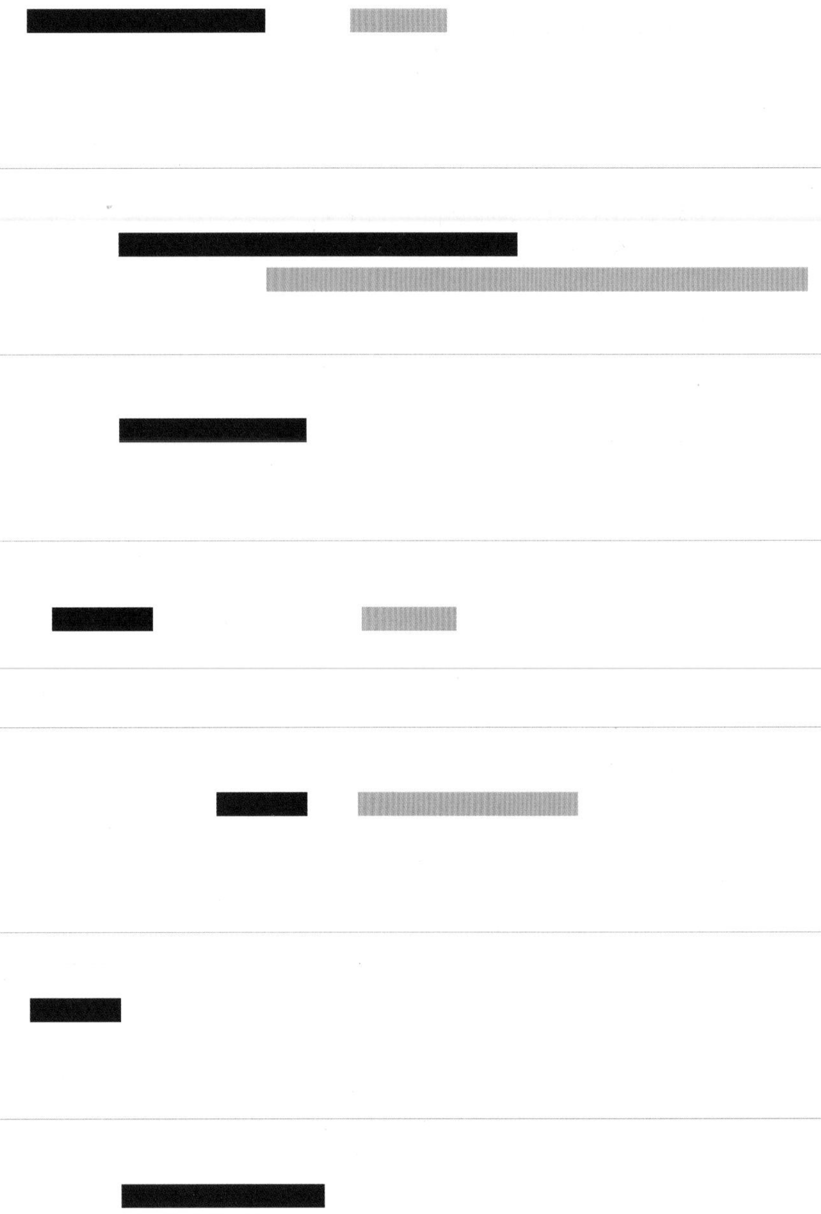

Flower Color & Season	Fruit/Foliage Color & Season	Height (in feet unless marked inches)	Water Requirements	Sun Requirements	Elevation (in feet)
Yellow (insignificant); spring	Bright red, fleshy cones, midsummer; **bluish gray-green stems attractive throughout the year**	4–6	Moderate watering to xeric	Full sun to partial shade	Up to 7,000
White; May–September	Pink, feathery tassels, summer–winter; **leaves nearly evergreen**	4–6	Moderate watering to dry	Full sun to partial shade	Up to 7,000
White to pink; May and June	Brown capsule; leaves bright green, deciduous	3–6	Moderate watering to dry	Sun to partial shade	Up to 10,000
Soft pink; early spring	Bright red berries, midsummer; leaves bluish green, deciduous	10–12	Moderate watering to dry	Full sun to partial shade	Up to 9,000
Pale yellow fading to pale orange; June	Red berries, midsummer–fall; leaves whitish green, circular terminal bracts silvery through fall, deciduous	8–12	Moderate watering	Full sun to partial shade	Up to 8,000
Green, inconspicuous; April	**Evergreen foliage**, with purple tints in winter	8–12 inches	Moderate watering	Partial shade to shade	Up to 7,000
White; May–July	Brown capsule; leaves dark blue-green, deciduous	6–8	Moderate watering to dry	Full sun to partial shade	Up to 8,000

Trees, Shrubs, and Woody Vines (Based upon information for Colorado USDA zone 5)

Scientific Name / Name used in trade* / page numbers	Flowering ▬ and Fruiting ▬ Seasons											
	SPRING			SUMMER			AUTUMN			WINTER		
	Apr	May	Jun	Jul	Aug	Sep	Oct	Nov	Dec	Jan	Feb	Mar
Prunus besseyi — Pawnee Buttes sand cherry — pages 42–43	▬	▬			▬							
Prunus nigra 'Princess Kay' — Princess Kay plum — pages 44–45	▬	▬			▬							
Rhamnus smithii — Smith's buckthorn — pages 46–47	▬	▬			▬	▬						
Ribes uva-crispa 'Red Jacket' — Comanche gooseberry — pages 48–49	▬	▬		▬	▬							▬
Sibiraea laevigata — Siberian spirea — pages 50–51			▬									
Viburnum ×rhytidophylloides 'Alleghany' — Alleghany viburnum — pages 52–53			▬		▬	▬	▬	▬				
Xanthoceras sorbifolium 'Psgan' — Clear Creek golden yellowhorn — pages 54–55	▬	▬			▬	▬	▬	▬				

Flower Color & Season	Fruit/Foliage Color & Season	Height (in feet unless marked inches)	Water Requirements	Sun Requirements	Elevation (in feet)
White; late April–May	Blue-black drupe, midsummer; leaves gray-green changing to maroon-red in fall, deciduous	15–18 inches	Moderate watering to dry	Full sun to partial shade	Up to 9,000
White, double; April–May	Yellowish red to red drupe, August; leaves dark green changing to yellow, orange or red in fall, deciduous	15–20	Moderate watering	Sun to partial shade	Up to 7,000
Greenish (nearly inconspicuous); April–May	Black berry, late summer; leaves green to yellowish green, deciduous	8–10	Moderate watering to dry	Full sun to partial shade	Up to 7,000
White to greenish pink; early spring	Red berries, midsummer; bright green, deciduous	2–3	Moderate watering	Full sun to partial shade	Up to 9,000
Greenish white with yellow centers; June	Brown follicle, July–late summer; bluish gray-green, deciduous	4–5	Moderate watering to dry	Full sun to partial shade	Up to 7,000
Creamy white; late May–early June	Reddish drupe changing to black, late August–fall; leaves dark green becoming purplish in winter, **deciduous to semi-persistent**	8–10	Moist soil to average	Sun to shade	Up to 7,000
White with blotch changing from yellow to red at base of throat; April–May	Green changing to brown, thick-walled capsule, late summer to fall; leaves lustrous green, deciduous	18–22	Moderate watering to xeric	Full sun to partial shade	Up to 6,000

Perennials (taller than 12 inches in height) (Based upon information for Colorado USDA zone 5)

Scientific Name / Name used in trade* / page numbers	Flowering ▬▬ Season											
	SPRING			**SUMMER**			**AUTUMN**			**WINTER**		
	Apr	May	Jun	Jul	Aug	Sep	Oct	Nov	Dec	Jan	Feb	Mar
Agastache aurantiaca CORONADO hyssop pages 58–59			▬▬▬	▬▬▬	▬▬▬	▬▬▬	▬					
Agastache cana 'Sinning'[PP13,673] SONORAN SUNSET hyssop pages 60–61					▬▬▬	▬▬▬	▬					
Agastache rupestris SUNSET hyssop pages 62–63				▬▬	▬▬▬	▬						
Aquilegia chrysantha DENVER GOLD columbine pages 64–65		▬▬	▬▬									
Aquilegia 'Swan Violet & White' REMEMBRANCE columbine pages 66–67		▬▬	▬▬									
Berlandiera lyrata Chocolate flower pages 68–69		▬▬	▬▬▬	▬▬▬	▬▬▬	▬▬						
Dianthus 'First Love' First Love dianthus pages 70–71	▬	▬▬▬	▬▬▬	▬▬	▬▬							
Diascia integerrima CORAL CANYON twinspur pages 72–73		▬▬	▬▬▬	▬▬▬	▬▬							
Digitalis obscura SUNSET foxglove pages 74–75			▬▬	▬								

Flower Color & Season	Foliage Color & Season	Height (in inches)	Water Requirements	Sun Requirements	Elevation (in feet)
Golden yellow and orange; summer–fall	Gray-green	15–18	Moderate watering to dry	Full sun to partial shade	Up to 7,000
Lavender-rose; late summer–fall	Gray-green	15–18	Moderate watering to dry	Full sun to partial shade	Up to 6,000
Sunset orange and mauve; late July–frost	Gray-green	20–24	Moderate watering to dry	Full sun to partial shade	Up to 7,000
Golden yellow; May–June	Blue-green	30–36	Moderate watering	Full sun to deep shade	Up to 9,000
Violet-purple spurs and white petals; late spring–early summer	Blue-green	14–24	Moderate watering	Partial sun	Up to 9,000
Ray: pale yellow above and red to maroon beneath (or at least on vein lines); Disk: red to maroon; May–September	Soft sage green to silvery gray	10–20	Minimal to no water once established	Full sun to partial shade	Up to 7,000
White changing to rosy pink; April–frost	Dark green; **basal leaves persist into winter**	15–20	Moderate watering	Sun to partial shade	Up to 10,000
Soft pink with deep pink throat; May–frost	Green	12–18	Moderate watering	Full sun to partial shade	Up to 7,000
Burnt sienna suffused with bright gold and reddish highlights; late June–August, with scattered blooms to frost	Green; **evergreen**	14–24	Moderate watering to dry	Full sun to partial shade	Up to 7,000

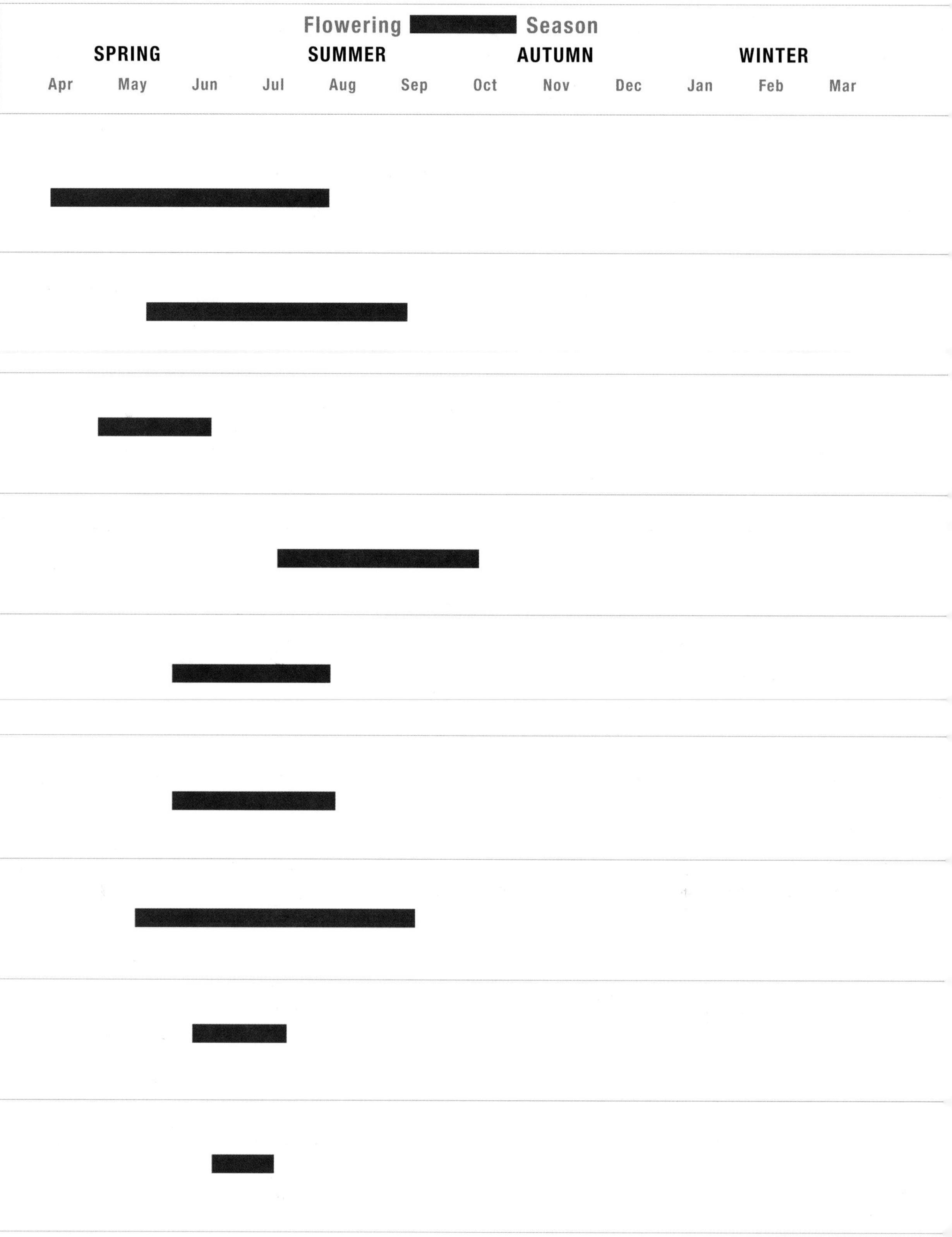

Scientific Name / Name used in trade* / page numbers	Flowering Season — SPRING			SUMMER			AUTUMN			WINTER		
	Apr	May	Jun	Jul	Aug	Sep	Oct	Nov	Dec	Jan	Feb	Mar
Digitalis thapsi — SPANISH PEAKS foxglove — pages 76–77	▬	▬	▬	▬	▬							
Epilobium fleischeri — Alpine willowherb — pages 78–79			▬	▬	▬	▬						
Penstemon grandiflorus — PRAIRIE JEWEL penstemon — pages 80–81		▬	▬									
Penstemon rostriflorus — Bridges' penstemon — pages 82–83				▬	▬	▬	▬					
Penstemon ×mexicali — PIKES PEAK PURPLE penstemon — pages 84–85			▬	▬	▬							
Penstemon ×mexicali — RED ROCKS penstemon — pages 86–87			▬	▬	▬							
Penstemon ×mexicali 'Psmeyers' — SHADOW MOUNTAIN penstemon — pages 88–89		▬	▬	▬	▬	▬						
Phlomis cashmeriana — Cashmere sage — pages 90–91			▬	▬								
Salvia argentea — Silver sage — pages 92–93			▬									

Flower Color & Season	Foliage Color & Season	Height (in inches)	Water Requirements	Sun Requirements	Elevation (in feet)
Raspberry; April–August	Green with yellow hairs	12–15	Moderate watering	Sun to partial shade	Up to 7,000
Delicate pink with red veins; late spring–fall	Gray-green	18–20	Moderate watering	Full sun to partial shade	Up to 8,000
Pure white through violet-purple; May–June	Bluish green	20–36	Moderate watering to dry	Full sun	Up to 8,000
Orange-red to scarlet; midsummer–fall	Green	24–36	Moderate watering to very dry	Full sun to partial shade	Up to 7,000
Vivid, violet-purple with white throat; June–August	Dark green	12–18	Moderate watering	Full sun to partial shade	Up to 7,000
Bright rosy red with white throat; June–August	Dark green	15–18	Moderate watering	Full sun to partial shade	Up to 7,000
Lavender-blue; May–September	Dark green	18–24	Moderate watering to xeric, once established	Full sun to partial shade	Up to 7,000
Lavender-pink; early summer	Light green	36–60	Moderate watering in sun to dry shade	Full sun to partial shade	Up to 7,000
White; early summer	Whitish light green	24–36 (when in flower); foliage less than 12	Average to dry, not too wet	Full sun to partial shade	Up to 8,000

Flowering ▬▬▬ Season

Scientific Name / Name used in trade* / page numbers	Apr	May	Jun	Jul	Aug	Sep	Oct	Nov	Dec	Jan	Feb	Mar
	SPRING			**SUMMER**			**AUTUMN**			**WINTER**		
Salvia darcyi 'Pscarl' — Vᴇʀᴍɪʟɪᴏɴ Bʟᴜꜰꜰs Mexican sage — pages 94–95					■	■	■					
Salvia greggii — Wild thing sage — pages 96–97			■	■	■	■	■					
Salvia greggii 'Furman's Red' — Furman's Red sage — pages 98–99			■	■	■	■	■					
Salvia pachyphylla — Mojave sage — pages 100–101			■	■	■	■	■					
Seseli gummiferum — Moon carrot — pages 102–103					■	■						
Spartina pectinata — Prairie cordgrass — Pages 104–105					■	■						
Sporobolus wrightii — Giant sacaton — Pages 106–107						■	■	■				

Flower Color & Season	Foliage Color & Season	Height (in inches)	Water Requirements	Sun Requirements	Elevation (in feet)
Brilliant cardinal red; August–October	Pastel green	35–40	Moderate watering	Full sun to partial shade	Up to 5,500
Hot pink to magenta; May–October	Light green	16–20	Moderate watering to xeric	Full sun to partial shade	Up to 6,000
Crimson to scarlet; June–October	Light green	18–24	Moderate watering to xeric	Full sun to partial shade	Up to 5,500
Violet-blue; June–November	Whitish green; **semi-evergreen**	18–36	Moderate watering to xeric	Full sun	Up to 5,500
Pale pink; midsummer–fall	Silvery blue	24–36	Moderate watering to xeric	Full sun to partial shade	Up to 5,000
Midsummer–fall	Light green; **brilliant yellow from fall to winter**	20–36 (when grown in water)	Best submerged in 1–6 inches of water	Full sun to partial shade	Up to 8,000
Late summer–fall	Light green; **golden from fall to winter**	60–72	Moderate watering to very dry	Full sun to partial shade	Up to 7,000

Perennial Groundcovers (Shorter than 12 inches in height)   (Based upon information for Colorado USDA Zone 5)

Scientific Name / Name used in trade* / page numbers	SPRING			SUMMER			AUTUMN			WINTER		
Flowering Season	Apr	May	Jun	Jul	Aug	Sep	Oct	Nov	Dec	Jan	Feb	Mar
Artemisia versicolor 'Sea Foam' — Sea Foam artemisia — pages 110–111		■	■									
Callirhoe involucrata — Winecups — pages 112–113	■	■	■	■	■	■						
Delosperma dyeri 'Psdold' — RED MOUNTAIN ice plant — pages 114–115	■	■	■	■	■	■						
Delosperma floribundum — Starburst ice plant — pages 116–117			■	■	■							
Delosperma 'John Proffitt' — TABLE MOUNTAIN ice plant — pages 118–119		■	■	■	■	■						
Delosperma 'Kelaidis'[PP13,876] — MESA VERDE ice plant — pages 120–121				■	■	■						
Epilobium canum subsp. *garrettii* — ORANGE CARPET hummingbird trumpet — pages 122–123					■	■						

Flower Color & Season	Foliage Color & Season	Height (in inches)	Water Requirements	Sun Requirements	Elevation (in feet)
Greenish-white (insignificant); April–June, scattered later	Silvery blue; **year-round appeal**	6–12	Moderate watering to dry	Full sun to partial shade	Up to 7,000
Wine red to magenta with white centers, fading to purple; April–hard frost	Rich dark blue-green with reddish tints in autumn	5–8	Moderate watering to dry	Full sun to partial shade	Up to 8,000
Burnished red petals with creamy center, fading to coppery red; April–September	Green, succulent; **year-round appeal**	2–3	Moderate watering to xeric once established	Full sun to partial shade	Up to 6,000
Shimmering, bright lilac-pink petals with white center; June–frost	Green, succulent; **year-round appeal**	2–4	Moderate watering to dry, not too wet	Full sun	Up to 8,000
Lustrous, fuchsia petals with white center; spring–fall	Green, tinged with purple in winter, succulent; **year-round appeal**	2–4	Moderate watering to dry	Sun to partial shade	Up to 7,000
Iridescent, salmon pink petals with a pale yellow center; summer–fall	Green, tinged with purple in winter, succulent; **year-round appeal**	2–4	Moderate watering to drier conditions	Full sun to partial shade	Up to 7,000
Bright red-orange to scarlet; mid–late summer	Whitish blue-green	4–6	Moderate watering to dry	Full sun to partial shade	Up to 9,000

Scientific Name Name used in trade* page numbers	Flowering ▬ Season											
	SPRING			**SUMMER**			**AUTUMN**			**WINTER**		
	Apr	May	Jun	Jul	Aug	Sep	Oct	Nov	Dec	Jan	Feb	Mar
Eriogonum umbellatum var. *aureum* 'Psdowns' KANNAH CREEK buckwheat pages 124–125		▬	▬									
Gazania krebsiana TANAGER gazania pages 126–127	▬	▬	▬	▬	▬	▬	▬				▬	
Gazania linearis COLORADO GOLD gazania pages 128–129	▬	▬	▬	▬	▬	▬	▬				▬	▬
Geranium magniflorum LA VETA LACE geranium pages 130–131		▬	▬									
Glandularia bipinnatifida VALLEY LAVENDER plains verbena pages 132–133		▬	▬	▬	▬							
Heuchera sanguinea 'Snow Angel' Snow Angel coral bells pages 134–135		▬										
Oenothera macrocarpa subsp. *incana* SILVER BLADE evening primrose pages 136–137		▬	▬	▬								

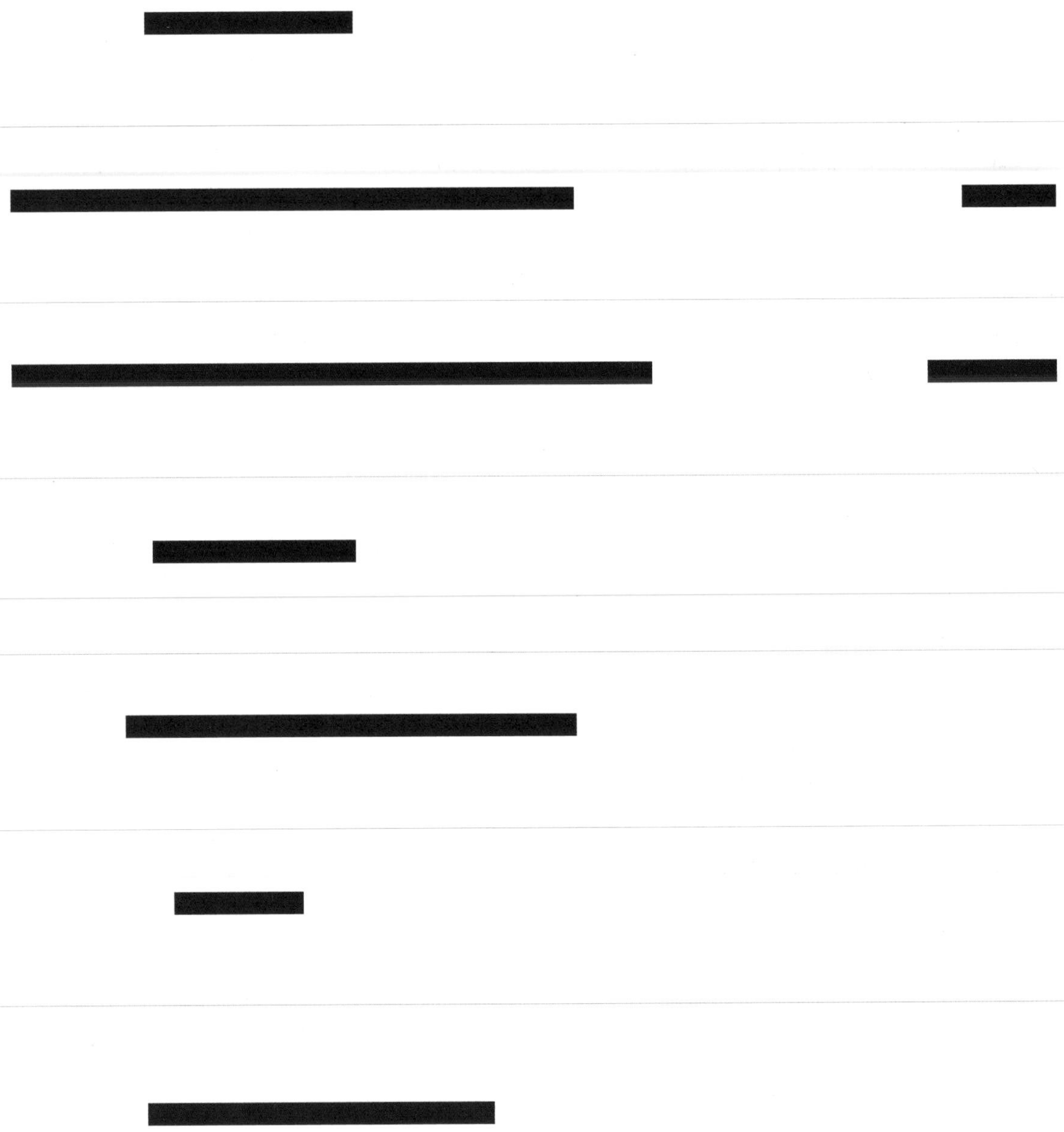

Flower Color & Season	Foliage Color & Season	Height (in feet unless marked inches)	Water Requirements	Sun Requirements	Elevation (in feet)
Sulfur yellow changing to orange, nearly red, May–July	Green changing to vivid purple-red in winter; **year-round appeal**	12–15	Moderate watering to xeric	Full sun to partial shade	Up to 10,000
Day-Glo orange with black spots at base of ray flowers; spring–fall	Dark green developing a deep purple tinge in winter; **year-round appeal**	4–6	Moderate watering to very dry	Full sun to partial shade	Up to 5,500
Ray: yellow with black basal spot; February–November	Deep green; **year-round appeal**	3–6	Moderate watering to dry	Full sun to partial shade	Up to 9,000
Vivid purple-lilac; late spring–midsummer	Green; **changing to scarlet or purple in early winter**	6–10	Moderate watering to dry	Full sun to partial shade	Up to 7,500
Bright, lavender-purple; May–October	Gray-green	3–6	Moderate watering to xeric	Full sun	Up to 6,000
Bright pink-red; late spring–summer	Green leaves marbled with light cream variegation	12–15 (when in flower)	Moderate watering	Partial sun to shade	Up to 8,000
Lemon yellow, may be mottled with red or change reddish with age; May–frost	Silvery gray-green	4–6	Moderate watering to dry	Full sun	Up to 8,000

Scientific Name Name used in trade* page numbers	Flowering ▬ Season											
	SPRING			**SUMMER**			**AUTUMN**			**WINTER**		
	Apr	May	Jun	Jul	Aug	Sep	Oct	Nov	Dec	Jan	Feb	Mar

Origanum libanoticum
Hopflower oregano
pages 138–139

Osteospermum barberiae var.
compactum
PURPLE MOUNTAIN sun daisy
pages 140–141

Osteospermum sp.
LAVENDER MIST sun daisy
pages 142–143

Penstemon linarioides subsp.
coloradoensis
SILVERTON bluemat penstemon
pages 144–145

Phlox bifida
SNOWMASS phlox
pages 146–147

Salvia daghestanica
PLATINUM sage
pages 148–149

Flower Color & Season	Foliage Color & Season	Height (in inches)	Water Requirements	Sun Requirements	Elevation (in feet)
Pinkish-lavender; summer–fall	Light bluish gray-green	10–15	Moderate watering	Full sun to partial shade	Up to 7,000
Ray: brilliant violet-red above, lighter beneath; Disk: purple; April–midsummer	Rich green	8–12	Moist to moderate watering	Full sun to partial shade	Up to 7,000
Ray: white changing to soft lavender; Disk: deep purple; spring and intermittently until fall.	Light green; **evergreen**	10–12	Moderate watering	Full sun to partial shade	Up to 7,000
Lavender-blue; May–June	Silvery blue-green, **evergreen**	8–12	Moderate watering to xeric	Full sun to partial shade	Up to 8,000
White; April–June	Dark green, **evergreen**	4–8	Moderate watering to dry	Full sun to partial shade	Up to 7,000
Dark blue; spring–early summer	Silvery green; **year-round appeal**	8–10	Moderate watering to xeric; good drainage	Full sun to partial shade	Up to 6,000

Scientific Name Name used in trade* page numbers	Flowering � Season											
	SPRING			SUMMER			AUTUMN			WINTER		
	Apr	May	Jun	Jul	Aug	Sep	Oct	Nov	Dec	Jan	Feb	Mar
Satureja montana subsp. *illyrica* Purple winter savory pages 150–151					▬	▬	▬					
Scutellaria suffrutescens Cherry skullcap pages 152–153				▬	▬	▬						
Veronica liwanensis Turkish veronica pages 154–155		▬	▬									
Veronica 'Reavis' Crystal River veronica pages 156–157		▬	▬									
Viola corsica Corsican violet pages 158–159	▬	▬	▬	▬	▬	▬	▬				▬	

Flower Color & Season	Foliage Color & Season	Height (in inches)	Water Requirements	Sun Requirements	Elevation (in feet)
Deep violet-lavender; August–October	Dark green; **situationally evergreen**	4–6	Moderate watering to xeric, once established	Full sun to partial shade	Up to 9,000
Cherry red; summer–fall	Whitish green	3–8	Moderate watering to dry	Full sun to partial shade	Up to 5,400
Cobalt blue; April–June	Dark green with purplish tints in winter; **evergreen**	1–2	Average to completely dry, once established	Full sun to partial shade	Up to 10,000
Pale blue with white throat; April–June, with scattered blooms thereafter	Dark green with purplish tints in winter; **evergreen**	2–3	Moderate watering to dry	Full sun to partial shade	Up to 8,000
Vivid violet-blue; early spring–late fall	Green	6–8	Moderate watering	Full sun to partial shade	Up to 9,000

Scientific Name Name used in trade* page numbers	Flowering ▬▬ and Fruiting ▭▭ Seasons											
	SPRING			SUMMER			AUTUMN			WINTER		
	Apr	May	Jun	Jul	Aug	Sep	Oct	Nov	Dec	Jan	Feb	Mar
Dolichos lablab 'Ruby Moon' Ruby Moon hyacinth bean pages 162–163			▬▬▬	▬▬▬	▬▬▭	▭						
Melinis nerviglumis PINK CRYSTALS ruby grass pages 164–165					▬▬▬	▬▬						
Plectranthus argentatus Silver dollar plant pages 166–167			▬▬▬	▬▬▬	▬							

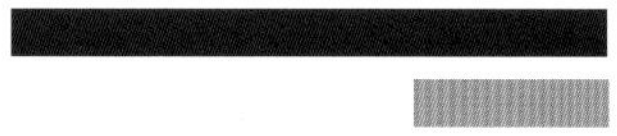

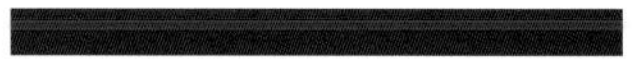

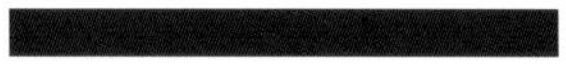

* Name used in commercial trade may be any one of the following: common name (e.g., fernbush); cultivated variety name (e.g., First Love dianthus); trademarked name, (e.g., PLATINUM sage); registered name, (e.g., PAWNEE BUTTES sand cherry).

** Bold-faced text in the Fruit/Foliage Color & Season and Foliage Color & Season columns hightlights desirable aspects of the foliage beyond the growing season, into late fall, winter, and early spring.

Flower Color & Season	Fruit/Foliage Color & Season	Height (in inches)	Water Requirements	Sun Requirements	Elevation (in feet)
Deep amethyst-violet; late spring to frost	Dark violet fruits, late summer; leaves dark purplish green	72–120 trellised; 36–60 untrellised	Moderate watering	Full sun to partial shade	Up to 7,000
Silvery pink; August to hard frost	Silvery pink achenes, August–hard frost; leaves pale bluish gray-green	20–24	Moderate watering	Full sun to partial shade	Up to 8,000
Bluish white (relatively insignificant); summer to frost	Leaves silver-green	20–36	Average to moderately dry	Full sun to partial shade	Up to 7,000

Silver dollar plant.

Acknowledgments

The information in this book is the culmination of more than two decades of hands-on gardening, long-term field trials, plant production protocol refinements, trade show demonstrations and educational programs, production and distribution of brochures, promotional articles in newspapers and magazines, and countless hours in meetings, by numerous individuals. It pays tribute to plant enthusiasts who dedicate their lives to gardening excellence and who have a mission to diversify the plant palette of the Rocky Mountains and High Plains. More than three years have passed since the idea of this book was conceived, and thousands of collective hours have been contributed in numerous ways to prepare it for publication. Plant Select's ad hoc book committee is to be commended for their vision for this documentary publication and for the management of this project. In addition, Denver Botanic Gardens' botanical illustration class members are to be lauded for the incalculable number of hours they contributed in creating the plant portraits showcased in this book. Denver Botanic Gardens, Colorado State University, and numerous members of the green industries of Colorado are recognized for their financial and philosophical support throughout the history of Plant Select. Plant Select is grateful to the individuals and organizations listed below for sharing their time and expertise toward the realization of *Durable Plants for the Garden*.

Editor
James E. Henrich

Art Direction and Graphic Design
Ann W. Douden, Fulcrum Publishing

Plant Select Board of Directors
Al Gerace, James E. Klett, Sarada Krishnan, Gene Pielin, Brian Vogt, Steve Wallner

Plant Select Marketing and Propagation Committees
Bill Adams, Joy Andrews, Ron Arpin, Betsy Baldwin-Owen, Heather Bennett, Mark Bickerstaff, Mike Bone, Jennifer Bousselot, Brian Core, Robert Cox, Kim Crowther, Gary Epstein, Ken Fisher, Steve Flickinger, Al Gerace, Ann Grant, Kelly Grummons, Harlan Hamernik, Leo Hartman, Butch Hartson, James E. Henrich, Shalene Hiller Navant, Beth Jacobson, Dan Johnson, Jerol Jones, Panayoti Kelaidis, Dale Kiyota, James E. Klett, Sarada Krishnan, Robert MacDonald, Harriett McMillan, Rich Meredith, Gene Milstein, John Navant, Patti Pfeifer, Gene Pielin, Diana Reavis, Kathy Rediske, David Salman, Irene Shonle, Duane Sinning, David Staats, Celia Tannehill, Mel Tessene, Cheryl Vestal, Larry Watson, David Winger, David Woodward, Susan Yetter, Frank Yantorno

Plant Select Ad Hoc Book Committee
James E. Henrich, Panayoti Kelaidis, James E. Klett, Harriett McMillan, Diana Reavis, Marcia Tatroe, Randy Tatroe, David Winger

Botanical Illustration Art Instructor
Susan T. Fisher

Botanical Illustrators
Claudia A. Anderson, Priscilla Baldwin, Janice H. Baucum, Karla Beatty, Stephanie Busby, Karen Cleaver, Beverly Coogan, Kathy Cranmer, Linda Darcy, Nancy N. DeGuire, Susan DiMarchi, Susan T. Fisher, Ann A. Fleming, Sharon Z. Garrett, Susan Halstedt, Sharon Hegner, Mervi Hjelmroos-Koski, Jayme S. Irvin, Renee L. Jorgensen, Libby Kyer, Martha J. Long, Donna Loomis, Susan G. Lyons, Debra Mallory, Melissa L. Martin, Jill Moring, Kate Hurley Morton, Susan B. Olson, Angela W. Overy, Sheila Payne, Sandra J. Penfound, Annie M. Reiser, Susan Rubin, Roy L. Sanford, Constance Sayas, Margaret A. Sjoden, Joan Sommerfeld, Julie Anne Sprinkle, Heidi Taylor, Julie Anne Terry, Janet C. Warren

Photographers
Ann Clark, Ray Daugherty, Pat Hayward, Robert Heapes, Shalene Hiller Navant, Mervi Hjelmroos-Koski, Dan Johnson, Panayoti Kelaidis, James E. Klett, Charles Mann, Harriett McMillan, Diana Reavis, Al Rollinger, Judy Sedbrook, David Staats, Randy Tatroe, David Winger, Susan Yetter

Content Contributors
Mark Bickerstaff, Mike Bone, Gary Epstein, Al Gerace, James E. Henrich, Shalene Hiller Navant, Dan Johnson, Panayoti Kelaidis, James E. Klett, Harriett McMillan, John Navant, Gene Pielin, Diana Reavis, Dr. Leila Shultz, Scott Skogerboe, Celia Tannehill, Dorothy P. Vance, Susan Yetter, Larry Watson

Administrative and Research Staff
Katy Derenzo, Gretchen DeWeese, Shalom Doty, Darlene Duran, Karen Elsner, Suzanne Gavin, Jeff Kinney, Meghan Loiz, Robert MacDonald, Tara Marquis, Donna Ralston, Julie Rudofsky, Bonnie Schilling, Diane Skogerboe, Kay Taylor

Information Resources
Deb Golanty at the Helen Fowler Library of Denver Botanic Gardens

Other Program Participants and Supporters
Chris Hartung, Plant Select Demonstration Gardens, Andrew Pierce, Ken Slump, The Denver Newspaper Agency, Gayle Weinstein

Bibliography

Agendae Academiae Sinicae (Edita). *Flora Reipublicae Popularis Sinicae.* Tomus 36: 67–70. Rosaceae (1): Spiraeoideae – Maloideae. Pekini (Beijing), China: Science Press, 1974.

Akhter, Rubina. *Flora of Pakistan, Caprifoliaceae.* No. 174. Islamabad, Pakistan: Pakistan Agricultural Research Council, 1986.

Arnold, T. H., and B. C. de Wet, eds. *Plants of Southern Africa: Names and Distribution.* Pretoria, South Africa: National Botanical Institute, 1993.

Bailey, L. H. *Hortus Third: A Concise Dictionary of Plants Cultivated in the United States and Canada.* New York: Macmillan, 1976.

Batten, Auriol. *Flowers of Southern Africa.* Sandton, South Africa: Frandsen Publishers, 1986.

Bean, W. J. *Trees & Shrubs Hardy in the British Isles.* 8th ed. rev. Vol. 4, Ri–Z. London: John Murray Ltd., 1980.

Bennet, Alfred W. *The Flora of the Alps.* Vol. 1. London: John C. Nimmo, 1896.

Bond, Pauline, and Peter Goldblatt. "Plants of the Cape Flora: A Descriptive Catalogue." Suppl. vol., *Journal of South African Botany* 13 (1984).

Castroviejo, S. (Coordinador General de la obra). *Flora Ibérica: Plantas Vasculares de la Península Ibérica e Islas Baleares.* Vol. 7 (1). Madrid, Spain: Real Jardín Botánico, CSIC, 1999.

Clebsch, Betsy. *A Book of Salvias: Sages for Every Garden.* Balmain, Australia: Florilegium, 1997.

Compton, Robert Harold. "The Flora of Swaziland." Suppl. vol., *Journal of South African Botany* 11 (1976).

Correll, Donovan S., Marshall C. Johnston, et al. *Manual of the Vascular Plants of Texas.* Renner, TX: Texas Research Foundation, 1970.

Cronquist, Arthur, Noel H. Holmgren, and Patricia K. Holmgren. *Intermountain Flora: Vascular Plants of the Intermountain West, U.S.A.* Vol. 3, pt. A. Bronx: New York Botanical Garden, 1997.

Dalziel, J. M. *The Useful Plants of West Tropical Africa.* London: Crown Agents for the Colonies, 1948.

Davis, P. H., ed. *Flora of Turkey and the East Aegean Islands.* Vol. 6. Edinburgh: Edinburgh at the Univ. Press, 1978.

———, ed. *Flora of Turkey and the East Aegean Islands.* Vol. 7. Edinburgh: Edinburgh at the Univ. Press, 1982.

Davis, Ray J., et al. *Flora of Idaho.* Provo, UT: Brigham Young Univ. Press, 1952.

Diggs, Jr., George M., Barney B. Lipscomb, and Robert J. O'Kennon. *Shinners & Mahler's Flora of North Central Texas.* Fort Worth: Botanical Research Institute of Texas and Austin College, 1999.

Dirr, Michael A. *Manual of Woody Landscape Plants: Their Identification, Ornamental Characteristics, Culture, Propagation and Uses.* Champagne, IL: Stipes Publishing, 1998.

Epling, Carl. "A Revision of *Salvia*, Subgenus *Calosphace.*" *Repertorium Specierum Novarum Regni Vegetabilis.* Band 110. Dahlem bei Berlin, Germany: Verlag des Repertoriums, 1939.

Facciola, Stephen. *Cornucopia: A Source Book of Edible Plants.* Vista, CA: Kampong Publications, 1990.

Gibbs Russell, G. E., et al. *Grasses of Southern Africa: An Identification Manual with Keys, Descriptions, Distributions, Classification, and Automated Identification and Information Retrieval from Computerized Data. Memoirs of the Botanical Survey of South Africa* No. 58. Pretoria, South Africa: National Botanic Gardens, 1991.

Gleason, Henry A. *The New Britton & Brown Illustrated Flora of the Northeastern United States and Adjacent Canada.* New York and London: Hafner, 1963.

Gleason, Henry A., and Arthur Cronquist. *Manual of Vascular Plants of Northeastern United States and Adjacent Canada.* Bronx: New York Botanical Garden, 1991.

Gledhill, Eily. *Eastern Cape Veld Flowers.* Cape Town, South Africa: The Department of Nature and Environmental Conservation of the Cape Provincial Administration, 1981.

Greuter, W., et al. *International Code of Botanical Nomenclature (Saint Louis Code).* Königstein, Germany: Koeltz Scientific Books, 2000.

Harden, Gwen J., ed. *Flora of New South Wales.* Vol. 3. Kensington, Australia: New South Wales Univ. Press, 1992.

Harrington, H. D. *Manual of the Plants of Colorado.* Chicago: Swallow Press, 1964.

Harvey, William H., and Otto Wilhelm Sonder. *Flora Capensis: Being a Systematic Description of the Plants of the Cape Colony, Caffraria, & Port Natal*. Vol. 3. Brook Nr. Ashford, England: L. Reeve & Co., 1894.

Hegi, Gustav. *Illustrierte Flora von Mitteleuropa*. Band 4, Teil 3. Berlin und Hamburg, Germany: Verlag Paul Parey, 1975.

———. *Illustrierte Flora von Mitteleuropa*. Band 5, Teil 2. Berlin und Hamburg, Germany: Verlag Paul Parey, 1975.

———. *Illustrierte Flora von Mitteleuropa*. Band 5, Teil 4. Berlin und Hamburg, Germany: Verlag Paul Parey, 1975.

Herre, H. *The Genera of the Mesembryanthemaceae*. Cape Town, South Africa: Tafelberg-Uitgewers Beperk, 1971.

Hiern, W. P. "Scrophulariaceae." In *Flora Capensis: Being a Systematic Description of the Plants of the Cape Colony, Caffraria, & Port Natal (and neighbouring territories)*. Vol. 4, sec. 2, edited by Sir William T. Thiselton-Dyer. London: Lovell Reeve & Co., 1904. Reprint, 1973.

Hilliard, O. M. *Compositae in Natal*. Pietermaritzburg, South Africa: Univ. of Natal Press, 1977.

Hsu, Ping-sheng, Jia-qi Hu, and Han-jin Wang. *Flora Reipublicae Popularis Sinicae*. Tomus 72: Caprifoliaceae. Pekini (Beijing), China: Science Press, 1988.

Huber, Herbert. *Illustrierte Flora von Mitteleuropa*. Band IV, Teil 2A. Berlin und Hamburg, Germany: Verlag Paul Parey, 1975.

Hutchinson, J., and J. M. Dalziel. *Flora of West Tropical Africa*. London: Crown Agents for Overseas Governments and Administrations, 1958.

Huxley, Anthony. *Mountain Flowers in Color*. New York: Macmillan, 1968.

Huxley, Anthony, Mark Griffiths, and Margot Levy, eds. *The New Royal Horticultural Society Dictionary of Gardening*. New York: Stockton Press/ London: Macmillan, 1992.

Ietswaart, J. H. *A Taxonomic Revision of the Genus* Origanum *(Labiatae)*. Leiden Botanical Series 4. The HagueNetherlands: Leiden Univ. Press, 1980.

Jacobsen, Hermann. *Lexicon of Succulent Plants*. London: Blandford Press, 1974.

Jacot Guillarmod, Amy. *Flora of Lesotho (Basutoland)*. Lehre, Germany: Verlag Von J. Cramer, 1971.

Jepson, Willis Linn. *A Manual of the Flowering Plants of California*. Berkeley: Univ. of California, 1925.

Kearney, Thomas H., et al. *The Flora of Arizona*. Berkeley and Los Angeles: Univ. of California Press, 1951.

Kelly, George W. *A Guide to the Woody Plants of Colorado*. Boulder, CO: Pruett Publishing Co., 1970.

Killick, Donald. *A Field Guide to the Flora of the Natal Drakensberg*. Johannesburg, South Africa: Johnathan Ball and Ad. Donker Publishers, 1990.

Komarov, V. L., and S. V. Yuzepchuk, eds. *Flora of the USSR*. Vol. 9, *Rosales and Sarraceniales*. Translated by Israel Program for Scientific Translations (1971). Movska-Lenningrad, Russia: Izdatel'stvo Akademii Nauk SSR, 1939.

Launert, E., and G. V. Pope. *Flora Zambesiaca*. Vol. 10, pt. 3. Whitstable (London): Managing Committee on Behalf of the Contributors to Flora Zambesiaca, 1989.

Law, Yuh-wu, et al. *Flora Reipublicae Popularis Sinicae*. Tomus 47 (1): Sapindaceae. Pekini (Beijing), China: Science Press, 1985.

Lawrence, George H. M. *Taxonomy of Vascular Plants*. New York: Macmillan, 1951.

Leonard, Emery C. "The North American Species of *Scutellaria*." *Contributions from the United States National Herbarium,* Vol. 22, pt. 10. Washington, DC: Government Printing Office, 1927.

Le Roux, A., and E.A.C.L.E. Schelpe. *South African Wild Flower Guide 1: Namaqualand and Clanwilliam*. Kirstenbosch, South Africa: Botanical Society of South Africa, 1981.

Le Roux, Annelise, and Ted Schelpe. *South African Wild Flower Guide 1: Namaqualand*. Kirstenbosch, South Africa: Botanical Society of South Africa, 1988.

Liguo, Fu, Yu Yongfu, and Harald Riedl. *Flora of China*. Vol. 4, *Cycadaceae through Fagaceae*. Beijing, China: Scientific Press/St. Louis: Missouri Botanical Garden, Scientific Publications, 1999.

Lowrey, T. K., and S. Wright, eds. *The Flora of the Witwatersrand*. Vol. 1, *The Monocotyledonae*. Johannesburg, South Africa: Witwatersrand Univ. Press, 1987.

Martin, W. C., and C. R. Hutchins. *A Flora of New Mexico*. Vaduz, Germany: A. R. Gantner Verlag KG, 1980.

Maytham Kidd, Mary. *South African Wild Flower Guide 3: Cape Peninsula*. Kirstenbosch, South Africa: Botanical Society of South Africa, 1983.

McGregor, Ronald L. "Onagraceae." In *Flora of the Great Plains*. Lawrence: Univ. Press of Kansas, 1986.

Meyers, Bruce. "A Summary of Bruce Meyers' *Penstemon* Hybridizations." *Bulletin of the American Penstemon Society* 57, no. 2 (1998): 2–11.

Moggi, Guido. *The Macdonald Encyclopedia of Alpine Flowers*. London: Macdonald & Co., 1985.

Moriarty, Audrey. *South African Wild Flower Guide 2: Outeniqua Tsitsikamma & Eastern Little Karoo*. Kirstenbosch, South Africa: Botanical Society of South Africa, 1982.

National Geographic Society. *National Geographic Family Reference Atlas of the World*. Washington, DC: National Geographic Society, 2002.

Onderstall, Jo. *South African Wild Flower Guide 4: Transvaal Lowveld and Escarpment Including the Kruger National Park*. Kirstenbosch, South Africa: Botanical Society of South Africa, 1984.

Pignatti, Sandro. *Flora D'Italia*. Vol. 2. Bologna, Italy: Edagricole, 1982.

Ping-tao, Li, and Anthony J. M. Leeuwenberg. *Flora of China*. Vol. 15, *Loganiaceae*. Beijing, China: Scientific Press/St. Louis: Missouri Botanical Garden, Scientific Publications, 1996.

Piper, Charles V. *Flora of the State of Washington: Contributions from the United States National Herbarium*. Vol. 11. Washington, DC: Government Printing Office, 1906.

"Plantae Lindheimerianae." *Boston Journal of Natural History.* Vol. 4, no. 2 (1850): 188–89.

Polunin, Oleg. *Flowers of Europe: A Field Guide*. London: Oxford Univ. Press, 1969.

Pooley, Elsa. *A Field Guide to Wild Flowers Kwazulu: Natal and the Eastern Region*. Durban, South Africa: Natal Flora Publications Trust, 1998.

Rand McNally and Company. *Rand McNally Premier World Atlas*. New census ed. Chicago/New York/San Francisco: Rand McNally, 1981.

Rechinger, Karl Heinz. *Flora Iranica*. No. 150, *Labiatae*. Graz, Austria: Akademische Druck – u. Verlagsanstalt, 1982.

Rehder, Alfred. *Manual of Cultivated Trees and Shrubs Hardy in North America*. 2nd ed. New York: Macmillan, 1940.

Rickett, William Harold. *Wild Flowers of the United States*. New York: McGraw-Hill, 1973.

Riedl, H. *Flora Iranica, Ephedraceae*. Graz, Austria: Akademische Druck – u. Verlagsanstalt, 1963.

Roessler, H. "Revision der Arctotideae – Gorteriinae (Compositae)." *Mitteilungen der Botanischen Staatssammlung München* 3 (1959): 71–500.

Ross, J. H. *The Flora of Natal, Republic of South Africa Department of Agricultural Technical Services Botanical Research Institute Botanical Survey Memoir* No. 39. Pretoria, South Africa: Government Printer, 1972.

Sanders, Roger W. *Taxonomy of* Agastache *Section* Brittonastrum *(Lamiaceae – Nepeteae)*. Systematic Botany Monographs 15. Ann Arbor, MI: The American Society of Plant Taxonomists, 1986.

Shearing, David. *South African Wild Flower Guide 6: Karoo*. Kirstenbosch, South Africa: Botanical Society of South Africa in Association with National Botanical Institute, 1994.

Shishkin, B. K., ed. *Flora of the U.S.S.R.* Vol. 21, *Labiatae*. Translated by Israel Program for Scientific Translations (1977). Movska-Lenningrad, Russia: Izdatel'stvo Akademii Nauk SSR, 1954.

Shreve, Forrest, and Ira L. Wiggins. *Vegetation and Flora of the Sonoran Desert*. Vol. 2. Stanford: Stanford Univ. Press, 1964.

Skogerboe, Scott. "Asexual Propagation of *Arctostaphylos ×coloradensis*." *The International Plant Propagators' Society Combined Proceedings* 53 (2003): 370–71.

Smith, Gideon F., et al. *Mesembs of the World: Illustrated Guide to a Remarkable Succulent Group*. Pretoria, South Africa: Briza Publications, 1998.

Stern, William T. *Botanical Latin: History, Grammar, Syntax, Terminology and Vocabulary*. Newton Abbot, England: David & Charles, 1978.

Steyermark, Julian A. *Flora of Missouri*. Ames: Iowa State Univ. Press, 1963.

Strausbaugh, P. D., and Earl L. Core. *Flora of West Virginia*. 2nd ed. Grantsville, WV: Seneca Books, 1977.

Strid, Arne. *Wild Flowers of Mount Olympus*. Kifissia, Greece: The Goulandris Natural History Museum, 1980.

Thomas, John Hunter. *Flora of the Santa Cruz Mountains of California: A Manual of the Vascular Plants*. Stanford: Stanford Univ. Press, 1961.

Tutin, T. G., et al., eds. *Flora Europaea*. Vol. 2. Cambridge: Cambridge Univ. Press, 1968.

———, eds. *Flora Europaea*. Vol. 3. Cambridge: Cambridge Univ. Press, 1972.

Valdés, Benito, Salvador Talavera, and Emilio Fernández-Galiano, eds. *Flora Vascular de Andalucía Occidental*. Barcelona, Spain: Ketres Editora, 1987.

van Jaarsveld, Ernst J. *Vygies: Gems of the Veld: A Garden and Field Guide to the South African Mesembs*. Venegono, Italy: Cactus & Co., 2000.

Wagner, Warren L. "New Species and Combinations in the Genus *Oenothera* (Onagraceae)." *Ann. Missouri Bot. Gard*. 70 (1983): 194–96.

Watson, Leslie and Michael Dallwitz. *The Grass Genera of the World*. Rev. ed. Wallingford, UK: CAB International, 1994.

Weber, William A. *Colorado Flora: Western Slope*. Boulder, CO: Colorado Associated Univ. Press, 1987.

Welsh, Stanley L., et al., eds. *A Utah Flora*. 3rd ed., rev. Provo, UT: Brigham Young Univ., 2003.

Wendelbo, P. *Flora Iranica*. No. 10, *Caprifoliaceae*. Graz, Austria: Akademische Druck – u. Verlagsanstalt, 1965.

Wiggins, Ira L. *Flora of Baja California*. Stanford: Stanford Univ. Press, 1980.

Willis, J. C. *A Dictionary of the Flowering Plants & Ferns*. 8th ed. Cambridge: Cambridge Univ. Press, 1985.

Wood, J. Medley. *A Handbook of the Flora of Natal*. Durban, South Africa: Bennett & Davies, 1907.

Yeo, Christine. *Salvias II*. Newton Abbot, England: Pleasant View Nursery/Wotton Printers, 1997.

Yeo, Peter F. *Hardy Geraniums*. 2nd ed. Portland, OR: Timber Press, 2002.

Internet Sites

Dave's Garden, *Artemisia versicolor,* http://davesgarden.com/guides/pf/go/64652/

The International Plant Names Index, www.ipni.org/index.html

Missouri Botanical Garden; w³TROPICOS, http://mobot.mobot.org/W3T/Search/vast.html

National Biological Information Infrastructure (NBII), http://159.189.176.5/portal/server.pt

Plants for a Future: Edible, Medicinal and Useful Plants for a Healthier World, *Xanthoceras sorbifolium,* www.pfaf.org/database/plants.php?Xanthoceras+sorbifolium

San Marcos Growers, *Salvia greggii* 'Furman's Red', www.smgrowers.com/products/plants/plantdisplay.asp?strLetter=S&plant_id=1436&page=

United States Forest Service, Fire Effects Information System, *Phildelphus lewisii,* www.fs.fed.us/database/feis/plants/shrub/philew/all.html, *Chamaebatiaria millefolium,*www.fs.fed.us/database/feis/plants/shrub/chamil/all.html, *Prunus besseyi* as *Prunus pumila* var. *besseyi,* www.fs.fed.us/database/feis/plants/shrub/prupum/all.html

University of Idaho Arboretum and Botanical Garden, *Philadelphus lewisii,* www.uidaho.edu/arboretum/june.html

USDA, Agricultural Research Service, Germplasm Resources Information Network (GRIN), www.ars-grin.gov/cgi-bin/npgs/html/index.pl

USDA Natural Resources Conservation Service, *Xanthoceras sorbifolia,* http://plants.usda.gov

Resources

Bailey, L. H. *The Manual of Cultivated Plants*. New York: Macmillan, 1966.

Ball, Ken, et al. *Taylor's Guide to Water-saving Gardening*. Boston: Houghton Mifflin, 1990.

Barr, Claude A. *Jewels of the Plains*. Minneapolis: Univ. of Minnesota Press, 1983.

Beaubaire, Nancy, ed. *Brooklyn Botanic Garden Native Perennials*. Brooklyn, NY: Brooklyn Botanic Gardens, 1996.

Bennett, Jennifer. *Dry-land Gardening: A Xeriscaping Guide for Dry-summer, Cold-winter Climates*. Willowdale, ON, Canada: Firefly Books, 1998.

Bird, Richard. *The Complete Book of Hardy Perennials*. London: Ward Lock, 1993.

Bloom, A. *Perennials for Your Garden*. Chicago: Floraprint U.S.A., 1981.

Bloom, Alan, and Adrian Bloom. *Blooms of Bressingham Garden Plants*. London: HarperCollins, 1992.

Brickell, Christopher, and Judith D. Zuk. *The American Horticultural Society A–Z Encyclopedia of Garden Plants*. New York: DK Publishing, 1997.

Brown, Lauren. *Grasses an Identification Guide*. Boston: Houghton Mifflin, 1979.

Carter, Brian, ed. *The Gardener's Palette*. New York: Doubleday, 1986.

Carter, Jack L. *Trees and Shrubs of Colorado*. Boulder, CO: Johnson Books, 1988.

Chatto, Beth. *Beth Chatto's Gravel Garden: Drought-resistant Planting through the Year*. New York: Penguin, 2000.

Clausen, Ruth Rogers, and Nicolas H. Ekstrom. *Perennials for American Gardens*. New York: Random House, 1989.

Coate, Barrie D. *Water-conserving Plants & Landscapes for the Bay Area*. Oakland, CA: East Bay Municipal Utility District, 1990.

Coates, Margaret Klipstein. *Perennials for the Western Garden*. Boulder, CO: Pruett Publishing, 1976.

Coombes, Allen J. *Dictionary of Plant Names*. Portland, OR: Timber Press, 1991.

Courtenay, Booth, and James H. Zimmerman. *Wildflowers and Weeds*. New York: Van Nostrand Reinhold, 1972.

Cox, R. A., and J. E. Klett. *Deciduous Shrubs for the Home Grounds*. Technical Bulletin SIA 7.415. Fort Collins, CO: Department of Horticulture, Colorado State Univ., 1988.

Creasy, Rosalind. *The Complete Book of Edible Landscaping*. San Francisco: Sierra Club Books, 1982.

Darke, R. *The Color Encyclopedia of Ornamental Grasses, Sedges, Rushes, Restios, Cattails, & Selected Bamboos*. Portland, OR: Timber Press, 1999.

Davis, Bryan. *Gardener's Illustrated Encyclopedia of Trees and Shrubs*. Emmaus, PA: Rodale Press, 1987.

Denver Water Department. *Designing Your Xeriscape: Plant Focus 1990*. Series 4, 1990.

———. *Xeriscape Plant Guide*. Golden, CO: Fulcrum Publishing, 1998.

DeWolf, Gordon P. *Taylor's Guide to Water-saving Gardening*. Boston: Houghton Mifflin, 1990.

DeWolf, Gordon P., ed. *Taylor's Guide to Shrubs*. Boston: Houghton Mifflin, 1987.

DeWolf, Gordon P., et al. *Taylor's Guide to Annuals*. Boston: Houghton Mifflin, 1986.

Dick-Peddie, William A., W. H. Moir, and R. Spellenberg. *New Mexico Vegetation: Past, Present and Future*. Albuquerque: Univ. of New Mexico Press, 1988.

Drew, John K. *Pictorial Guide to Hardy Perennials*. Kalamazoo, MI: Merchants Publishing Co., 1984.

Dunmire, John R., et al., eds. *Sunset Western Garden Book*. Menlo Park, CA: Lane Magazine and Book Co., 1971.

Elias, Thomas S. *The Complete Trees of North America: Field Guide and Natural History*. New York: Times Mirror Magazines, 1980.

Ellefson, C., T. Stephens, and D. Welsh. *Xeriscape Gardening: Water Conservation for the American Landscape*. New York: Macmillan, 1992.

Ellefson, Connie Lockhart, and David Winger. *Xeriscape Colorado: The Complete Guide*. Englewood, CO: Westcliffe Publishers, 2004.

Elliot, J. *The Smaller Perennials*. Portland, OR: Timber Press, 1997.

Elmore, Francis H. *Shrubs and Trees of the Southwest Uplands*. Tucson, AZ: Southwest Parks and Monuments Assn., 1976.

Fairchild, D. H., and J. E. Klett. *Woody Landscape Plants for the High Plains*. Technical Bulletin LTB93-1. Fort Collins, CO: Department of Horticulture, Colorado State Univ., 1993.

Feldman, Fran, and Cornelia Fogle, eds. *Sunset Waterwise Gardening*. Menlo Park, CA: Lane Publishing Co., 1989.

Ferguson, Nicole. *Right Plant, Right Place*. New York: Summit Books, 1984.

Feucht, James R. *Xeriscaping: Trees and Shrubs for Low-water Landscapes*. Technical Bulletin SIA 7.229. Fort Collins, CO: Department of Horticulture, Colorado State Univ., 1987.

Gerhold, Henry D., et al., eds. *Street Tree Factsheets*. Univ. Park: Penn State College of Agricultural Sciences, 1993.

Greenlee, John. *The Encyclopedia of Ornamental Grasses: How to Grow and Use Over 250 Beautiful and Versatile Plants.* New York: Michael Friedman Publishing Group, 1992.

Grounds, R. *The Plantfinder's Guide to Ornamental Grasses*. Portland, OR: Timber Press, 1998.

Harrington, H. D. *Edible Native Plants of the Rocky Mountains*. Albuquerque: Univ. of New Mexico Press, 1967.

————. *Manual of the Plants of Colorado*. Chicago: Swallow Press, 1964.

Hightshoe, Gary L. *Native Trees for Urban and Rural America*. Ames: Iowa State Univ. Foundation, 1978.

Holmes, Roger, ed. *Taylor's Guide to Natural Gardening*. Boston: Houghton Mifflin, 1993.

Huxley, Anthony, Mark Griffiths, and Margot Lery, eds. *The New Royal Horticulture Society Dictionary of Gardening*. London: Macmillan, 1992.

Jescavage-Bernard, Karen. "Berried in the Snow." *National Gardening* 14 (1991): 40–44.

Kelley, George W. *Shrubs for the Rocky Mountains*. Cortez, CO: Rocky Mountain Horticultural Publishing Co., 1979.

————. *Trees for the Rocky Mountains*. Cortez, CO: Rocky Mountain Horticultural Publishing Co., 1976.

Kingsbury, John M. *Poisonous Plants of the United States*. Englewood Cliffs, NJ: Prentice Hall, 1964.

Knopf, Jim. *The Xeriscape Flower Gardener, Water-wise Guide for the Rocky Mountain Region*. Boulder, CO: Johnson Books, 1991.

Knox, Gerald M., et al., eds. *Better Homes and Gardens Complete Guide to Gardening*. Des Moines, IA: Meredith Corp., 1980.

Lampe, Kenneth, and Mary Ann McCann. *AMA Handbook of Poisonous and Injurious Plants*. Chicago: American Medical Assn., 1985.

Lenhart, Frederick W. *Trees and Shrubs Identified*. Denver: Lenhart, 1980.

Little, Elbert. *The Audubon Society Field Guide to North American Trees, Western Region*. New York: Alfred A. Knopf, 1980.

Lowe, D. *Cushion Plants for the Rock Garden*. Portland, OR: Timber Press, 1995.

MacKenzie, David S. *Complete Manual of Perennial Ground Covers*. Englewood Cliffs, NJ: Prentice Hall, 1989.

Macoboy, Stirling. *What Flower Is That?* New York: Portland Home, 1986.

Maino, Evelyn, and Frances Howard. *Ornamental Trees: An Illustrated Guide to Their Selection and Care*. Berkeley: Univ. of California Press, 1955.

McGary, Jane, ed. *Rock Garden Plants of North America – An Anthology from the Bulletin of North American Rock Garden Society*. Portland, OR: Timber Press, 1996.

McGregor, Ronald. *Flora of Great Plains*. Kansas City: Kansas Univ. Press, 1986.

McKean, William T., ed. *Winter Guide to Central Rocky Mountain Shrubs*. Denver: State of Colorado Department of Natural Resources Division of Wildlife, 1976.

McPherson, E. Gregory, and Gregory H. Graves. *Ornamental and Shade Trees for Utah: A Tree Guide for Intermountain Communities*. Logan: Cooperative Extension Service of Utah State Univ., 1984.

Nelson, Ruth Ashton. *Handbook of Rocky Mountain Plants*. Estes Park, CO: Skyland Publishers, 1979.

————. *Plants of Rocky Mountain National Park*. Estes Park, CO: Rocky Mountain Nature Assn., 1982.

Noland, D. A., and K. Bolin. *Perennials for the Landscape*. Danville, IL: Interstate Publishers, 2000.

Nold, R. *Penstemons*. Portland, OR: Timber Press, 1999.

Normand Matheson, Suzanne, ed. *Sunset Perennials*. Menlo Park, CA: Sunset Publishing Corp., 1992.

Norris Brenzel, Kathleen, ed. *Sunset Western Garden Book*. Menlo Park, CA: Sunset Publishing Corp., 1995.

Pesman, M. Walter. *Meet the Natives: The Amateur's Field Guide to Rocky Mountain Wildflowers, Trees, and Shrubs*. 9th ed. Boulder, CO: Roberts Rinehart Publishers, 1992.

Phillips, Judith. *Southwestern Landscaping with Native Plants*. Santa Fe: Museum of New Mexico Press, 1987.

Pirone, Pascal P. *Diseases and Pests of Ornamental Plants*. New York: John Wiley and Sons, 1978.

Preston, Jr., Richard J. *North American Trees*. Cambridge: Massachusetts Institute of Technology, 1965.

———. *Rocky Mountain Trees*. New York: Dover Publications, 1968.

Rice, G. *Hardy Perennials*. Portland, OR: Timber Press, 1995.

Rickett, William Harold. *Wild Flowers of the United States*. New York: McGraw-Hill, 1973.

Robinette, G. O. *Plants, People and Environmental Quality*. No. 2405-0479. Prepared for the US Department of the Interior, National Parks Service. Washington, DC: US Government Printing Office, 1972.

Rondon, Joanne. *Landscaping for Water Conservation in a Semi-arid Environment*. Aurora, CO: City of Aurora, 1980.

Sajeva, M., and M. Costanzo. *Succulents: The Illustrated Dictionary*. Portland, OR: Timber Press, 1994.

Seymour, E. L. D. *The Wise Garden Encyclopedia*. New York: HarperCollins, 1990.

Sinclair, Wayne A., et al. *Diseases of Trees and Shrubs*. Ithaca, NY: Cornell Univ. Press, 1987.

Sinnes, A. Cort. *All About Annuals*. San Francisco: Ortho Books, 1981.

Spellenberg, Richard. *The Audubon Society Field Guide to North American Wildflowers: Western Region*. New York: Alfred A. Knopf, 1979.

Springer, Lauren. *The Undaunted Garden*. Golden, CO: Fulcrum Publishing, 1994.

Still, Steven. *Herbaceous Ornamental Plants*. Champaign, IL: Stipes Publishing Co., 1982.

———. *Manual of Herbaceous Plants*. Champaign, IL: Stipes Publication Co., 1994.

Strauch, Jr., Joseph G., and James E. Klett. *Flowering Herbaceous Perennials for the High Plains*. Technical Bulletin LTB89-5. Fort Collins, CO: Department of Horticulture, Colorado State Univ., 1989.

Sunset New Western Garden Book. Menlo Park, CA: Lane Publishing, 1979.

Tannehill, Celia, and James E. Klett. *Best Perennials for the Rocky Mountains and High Plains*. Technical Bulletin 573A. Fort Collins, CO: Colorado State Univ. Cooperative Extension, 2002.

Tatroe, Marcia. *Cutting Edge Gardening in the Intermountain West*. Boulder, CO: Johnson Books, 2007.

———. *Perennials for Dummies: A Reference for the Rest of Us!* Foster City, CA: IDG Books, 1997.

Taylor, Jane. *Drought-tolerant Plants, Waterwise Gardening for Every Climate*. New York: Prentice Hall, 1993.

Taylor, Norman. *Taylor's Guide to Gardening*. Cambridge, MA: Riverside Press, 1948.

Trelease, William. *Plant Materials of Decorative Gardening: Identification of Trees and Shrubs*. New York: Dover Publications, 1968.

Turner, R. J., and Ernie Wasson, eds. *Botanica: The Illustrated A–Z of Over 10,000 Garden Plants and How to Cultivate Them*. 2nd ed. Milsons Point, Australia: Mynah/Random House Australia Pty Ltd., 1998.

United States Department of Agriculture. *Trees: The Yearbook of Agriculture 1949*. Washington, DC: US Government Printing Office, 1949.

Venning, Frank D. *Wildflowers of North America*. New York: Golden Press, 1984.

Watson, Larry E. "Favorite Water-wise Trees and Shrubs." *Mountain, Plain, and Garden* 49 (1992): 22–24.

Way, D., and P. James. *The Gardener's Guide to Growing Penstemons*. Portland, OR: Timber Press, 1998.

Weber, William A. *Rocky Mountain Flora*. Boulder, CO: Colorado Assoc. Univ. Press, 1976.

Whitson, Tom D., et al., eds. *Weeds of the West*. Cheyenne, WY: The Western Society of Weed Science, in cooperation with the Western United States Land Grant Universities Cooperative Extension Services and the Univ. of Wyoming, 1991.

Selected references reprinted with permission from Colorado State University Extension, *Best Perennials for the Rocky Mountains and High Plains* by Celia Tannehill and James E. Klett, ISBN 1-889143-09-X, and Denver Water Department, *Xeriscape Plant Guide*. Golden, CO: Fulcrum Publishing, 1998.

Additional Resources

Visit the Plant Select website, www.plantselect.org, for the most current information about the program and plant promotions. It features:

Plant Profiles: A complete inventory of all Plant Select plants, featuring descriptions, cultural requirements, and color images.

Plant Sources: Locate garden centers near you with addresses and contact information for member companies that sell Plant Select plants.

Demonstration Gardens: Discover treasure troves of beauty at these participating gardens. Addresses, contact information, and an overview map are provided for your convenience.

Glossary

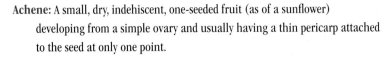

Achene: A small, dry, indehiscent, one-seeded fruit (as of a sunflower) developing from a simple ovary and usually having a thin pericarp attached to the seed at only one point.

Alkaline: Basic, especially of a solution having a pH of more than 7.

Amendment: A material (such as compost) that aids plant growth, either directly or indirectly, by improving the condition of the soil.

Annual: Plants completing their life cycle in one growing season.

Anther: The part of a stamen of a seed plant that produces and contains pollen.

Aril: An appendage or an outer covering of a seed, growing out from the point of seed attachment; sometimes it appears as a pulpy covering.

Armed: Provided with any kind of strong or sharp defense, as of thorns, spines, prickles, barbs.

Axis: A plant stem.

Basal: Arising from the base of the stem (leaves).

Beak: A long, prominent, and substantial point; applied particularly to prolongations of fruits and pistils.

Berry: Pulpy, indehiscent, few- or many-seeded fruit; technically, the pulpy fruit resulting from a single pistil, containing one or more seeds but no true stone, as the tomato or grape.

Biennial: Plants that grow vegetatively during the first year, then fruit and die during the second.

Bract: A leaf borne on a floral axis, especially one subtending a flower or flower cluster.

Bracteole: A secondary bract; a bractlet.

Broadleaf evergreen: A term used to describe nonconiferous trees and shrubs that bear persistent broad green leaves, as opposed to needles.

Burl: A kind of knot on some tree trunks.

Caespitose: Matted; growing in tufts; in little dense clumps; said of low plants that make tufts or turf of their basal growth.

Calcareous: Growing on limestone or in soil impregnated with lime.

Calyx; Calices: The usually green or leaflike part of a flower comprised collectively of all of the sepals.

Cambium tissue: Thin layer of living tissue between the bark and wood of woody plants, produces new layers of bark and wood.

Canescent: Covered with downy gray hairs.

Capsule: A dry fruit resulting from the maturing of a compound ovary (of more than one carpel), usually opening at maturity along one or more sutures.

Cardiotonic: Relating to or having a favorable effect upon the action of the heart.

Carpel: An ovule-bearing unit of an ovary.

Caudex: Stem.

Cauline: Pertaining or belonging to an obvious stem or axis, as opposed to basal or rosulate.

Chance-seedling: A random seedling that develops into a plant with characteristics atypical for the species.

Cinereous: Ash-colored; light gray.

Clone: A group of individuals resulting from vegetative multiplication; any plant propagated vegetatively and therefore presumably a duplicate of its parent. Originally spelled *clon*, but changed to *clone* by its coiner (H. J. Webber); proposed in application to horticultural varieties.

Connate-perfoliate: Said of opposite leaves without petioles, united by their bases, the axis seemingly passing through them.

Coriaceous: Of leathery texture.

Corolla: The petals of a flower, collectively; the petals can be identical and separate (e.g., magnolia); modified (e.g., pea); fused partially (e.g., bellflower); fused completely like a funnel (e.g., morning glory); or fused and modified (e.g., snapdragon).

Cotyledon: The first leaf or one of the first pair or whorl of leaves developed by the embryo of a seed plant or of some lower plants.

Crenate: Shallowly round-toothed or obtusely toothed, scalloped.

Cross-pollination: Transfer of pollen from one flower to the stigma of a flower on another plant with a different genetic makeup.

Crown: The highest part (as of a tree).

Culm: A monocotyledonous stem (as of a grass or sedge).

Cultivar: A category of plants that are, firstly, below the level of a subspecies taxonomically, and, secondly, found only in cultivation. It is an international term denoting certain cultivated plants that are clearly distinguishable from others by stated characteristics and that retain their distinguishing characters when reproduced under specific conditions, thereby requiring a name. Cultivar names are now formed from not more than three words in a modern language and are usually distinguished typographically by the use of single quotation marks, as *Vaccinium macrocarpon* cultivar (cv.) 'Early Black'. The word is derived from "cultivated" + "variety" and abbreviated cv.

Cutting: A piece of a plant able to grow into a new plant.

Cyme: An inflorescence in which each floral axis terminates in a single flower.

Cymule: Dimutive of cyme, usually few-flowered.

Deadhead: To remove the faded flowers from a plant, especially to keep a neat appearance and to promote reblooming by preventing seed production.

Deciduous: Leaves falling off, usually at the end of a period of growth or in response to environmental stress (e.g., insufficient water, excessive heat).

Decumbent: Reclining or lying on the ground, but with the end ascending.

Dehisce: To discharge contents by splitting (seed pods dehisce at maturity).

Deltoid: Triangular; deltalike.

Denticulate: With minute or fine sharp indentations or teeth that are perpendicular to the margin, usually referring to a leaf margin.

Disk flower: The tubular flowers in the center of the heads of most sunflower family members, as distinguished from the peripheral ray flowers, when present (e.g., the flowers comprising the center of a sunflower head).

Drupe: A partly fleshy, one-seeded fruit (as a plum or cherry) that remains closed at maturity.

Ecotone: A transition zone between two or more ecosystems.

Ectomycorrhizal fungi: Fungi that form symbiotic relationships on the roots of host plants.

Elliptic: Oval in outline, narrowed to rounded ends, and widest at or about the middle.

Endemic: Native or confined naturally to a particular and usually restricted area or region; biologically a relic of once wide distribution.

Erose: Said of a margin when appearing eroded or gnawed or of a jaggedness too small to be fringed or too irregular to be toothed.

Evergreen: Having foliage that remains green (most coniferous trees).

Exfoliating: Peeling off in shreds, thin layers, or plates, as bark from a tree trunk or shrub stem.

Farinaceous: Containing starch or starchlike materials; sometimes applied to a surface covered with a mealy coating, as leaves of some *Primula* spp.; farinose.

Floccose: Covered with tufts of soft woolly hairs that usually rub off readily.

Foliate buds: Buds that are large and leaflike; giving a plant the impression of being evergreen.

Germplasm: The substance in germ cells by which hereditary characteristics are believed to be transmitted.

Glabrate/glabrescent: Nearly glabrous, or becoming glabrous with maturity or age.

Glabrous: Not hairy; often incorrectly used to mean "smooth."

Glaucous: Covered with a bloom, or whitish substance, that rubs off.

Groundcover: A planting of low plants (as ivy) that covers the ground in place of turf. A plant adapted for use as a groundcover.

Gymnosperm: A plant lacking flowers and reproducing by seeds borne naked on a special bract or sporophyll, most often in a cone, in contrast to the angiosperms, which have flowers and have seeds enclosed in (mature) ovaries.

Hardy annual: A plant with only one growing season that demonstrates vigorous good health and is capable of withstanding adverse growing conditions.

Head: A short dense spike, characteristic of the sunflower family.

Hell strip: A narrow planting bed, typically surrounded by concrete or asphalt, completely exposed to the elements and extremely challenging to maintain.

Herbaceous: Of a stem: having little or no woody tissue and persisting usually for a single growing season.

Hoary: Covered with close white or whitish hairs.

Hybrid: A plant resulting from a cross between parents that are genetically unlike; more commonly, in descriptive taxonomy, the offspring of two different species or their infraspecific units.

Indehiscent: Remaining closed at maturity.

Indeterminate: Characterized by sequential flowering from the lateral or basal buds to the central or uppermost buds; also: characterized by growth in which the main stem continues to elongate indefinitely without being limited by a terminal inflorescence.

Indumentum: A rather heavy hairy, or pubescent, covering.

Inflorescence: The manner of development and arrangement of flowers on a stem; also, a flowering stem with its appendages comprising a flower cluster.

Lanceolate: Lance shaped; much longer than broad; widening above the base and tapering to the apex.

Latex: Milky sap.

Layering: A shoot of a living plant bent down and partly covered with soil so that it may take root.

Leaf axil: The angle between a branch or leaf and the axis from which it arises.

Leaflet: One part of a compound leaf; secondary leaf.

Legume: Simple fruit dehiscing on both sutures, characteristic of bean family members.

Lenticel: A loose aggregation of cells that penetrates the surface (as of a stem) of a woody plant and through which gases are exchanged between the atmosphere and the underlying tissues.

Limb: The expanding free and unfused part(s) of a partially tubular or fused flower, often appearing as the tips of petals.

Linear: Long and narrow, the sides parallel or nearly so, as blades of most grasses.

Lip: One of the parts in an unequally divided corolla or calyx; there are usually two parts, the upper lip and the lower lip, although one lip is sometimes wanting; the upper lip of orchids is by a twist of the ovary made to appear as the lower; a labium.

Loam: A loose soil of mixed clay, sand, and silt.

Lyrate: Cleft or parted in a pinnate (featherlike) way, but with an enlarged terminal lobe and smaller lower lobes.

Marcescent: Withering, but the remains persisting.

Mericarp: One-half of a schizocarp.

Monotypic: In reference to a genus, composed of a single species.

Nectariferous: Bearing or possessing an abundance of nectar.

Nutlet: A small or diminutive nut; nucule; similar to an achene but with a harder and thicker wall.

Oblanceolate: The reverse of lanceolate: a leaf broader at the distal third than at the middle and tapering toward the base.

Obovate: The opposite of ovate, the terminal half broader than the basal.

Ochrea: A sheath that encircles a stem at the node, or point of leaf attachment, often papery; characteristic of the buckwheat family (e.g., rhubarb) (also spelled *ocrea*).

Ovary: Ovule-bearing part of a pistil.

Ovate: With an outline like that of hen's egg, the broader end below the middle.

Palmate: Lobed or divided or ribbed in a palmlike or handlike fashion; digitate, although this word is usually restricted to compound leaves rather than to merely ribbed or lobed leaves.

Panicle: A branched flower cluster (as of a lilac) in which each branch from the main stem has one or more flowers.

Papillose (Papillate): Bearing minute pimplelike protuberances (papillae).

Peduncle: Stalk of a flower cluster or of a solitary flower when that flower is the remaining member of an inflorescence.

Perennial: Continuing to live from year to year.

Perfoliate: Descriptive of a sessile leaf or bract whose base completely surrounds the stem, the latter seemingly passing through the leaf.

Pergola: A structure consisting of posts supporting an open roof in the form of a trellis.

Petiole: A slender stem that supports a leaf.

pH: A measure of acidity and alkalinity of a solution that is a number on a scale on which a value of 7 represents neutrality and lower numbers indicate increasing acidity and higher numbers increasing alkalinity.

Pinnate: Resembling a feather, especially in having similar parts arranged on opposite sides of an axis, like the barbs on the rachis of a feather.

Pistil: The female part of a flower, comprised of ovary, style, and stigma.

Plant patent: Two distinct forms of plant patent or patentlike protection are available for new plant varieties: (a) 1930 Plant Patent Act (PPA), PTO (US Patent and Trademark Office) may grant patents for asexually reproduced varieties and (b) under the 1970 Plant Variety Protection Act (PVPA) protection of new sexually reproduced varieties are protected by the Department of Agriculture and designated by the abbreviation *PP* plus a number.

Primed seed: Seeds are said to have been primed after being subjected to water absorption levels that stimulate the metabolic events associated with germination, stopping short of radicle emergence. Primed seeds demonstrate enhanced germination speed and greater uniformity.

Procumbent: Being or having stems that trail or lie flat along the ground without rooting.

Propagate: To reproduce or cause to reproduce sexually by seeds, or asexually from cuttings, corms, bulbs, rhizomes, tubers, or divisions.

Propagule: A structure with the capacity to give rise to a new plant, for example, a seed, a spore, or a part of the vegetative body capable of independent growth if detached from the parent.

Puberulent: Minutely pubescent; the hairs soft, straight, erect, scarcely visible to the unaided eye.

Pubescent: Covered with short, soft hairs; downy.

Raceme: A simple, elongated, indeterminate inflorescence with pedicelled, or stalked, flowers.

Ray flower: Outer modified floret (flower) of some sunflower family members having the appearance of a petal (e.g., outer colorful flowers of a sunflower).

Rejuvenation pruning: To periodically prune out old stems or canes to encourage new, vigorous growth.

Resinous: Containing or producing resin, said of bud scales when coated with a sticky exudate of resin (as in *Aesculus* spp.).

Revolute: Rolled backward; with margin rolled toward lower side.

Rhizomatous: Producing or possessing rhizomes.

Rhizome: A fleshy, rootlike, and usually horizontal, underground plant stem that forms shoots above and roots below.

Rosette: An arrangement of leaves radiating from a crown or center and usually at or close to the earth, as in *Taraxacum* (dandelion).

Rosulate: Rosette shaped.

Rudimentary: Imperfectly developed and nonfunctional.

Samara: An indehiscent, winged fruit, as of an ash, elm, or maple.

Scapose: Bearing flowers on a leafless stem arising from the ground.

Scarify: To mechanically (cut, nick, or chip) or chemically (as with an acid) soften the hard or thick wall of a seed allowing more rapid absorption of water to hasten germination.

Schizocarp: A dry dehiscent fruit that splits into two halves, each half called a mericarp, as in most members of the carrot family, or in maples.

Secund: One-sided; said of inflorescences when the flowers appear as if borne from only one side.

Sepal: One of the separate parts of a calyx, usually green and leaflike.

Sericeous: Silky.

Serrulate: Said of a margin that is minutely saw-toothed with the teeth pointing forward.

Sessile: Not stalked.

Shelterbelt: A barrier of trees and shrubs that provides protection from wind and storms and reduces erosion.

Spatulate: Spoon shaped.

Specimen plant: A plant with meritorious characters that warrants being featured (in the landscape or in a container) as an individual, worthy of being viewed from all angles.

Spicate: Spikelike.

Spikelet: A secondary spike; one part of a compound inflorescence which of itself is spicate; the floral unit, or ultimate cluster, or a grass inflorescence composed of flowers and their subtending bracts.

Sporophyll: A leaflike organ bearing reproductive parts or organs.

Sport: A mutation resulting in a visible change to the typical morphology of a plant; such changed parts must generally be propagated vegetatively and not from seeds.

Squamulate: Bearing or possessing a squamula, or small lobe.

Stigma: The part of the pistil of a flower that receives the pollen grains and on which they germinate.

Stipule: A basal appendage of a petiole; the three parts of a complete leaf are blade, petiole, stipules (usually two).

Stolon: A horizontal, basal stem at or below the surface of the ground that produces new plants from buds at its tip or nodes; also called a runner.

Stratification: Often called moist-chilling, stratification involves soaking dry seeds for twelve to twenty-four hours, draining them, mixing them with a moisture-retaining medium, and storing them for a specified period at 35° to 45°F. The treatment is most often required to germinate seeds of woody trees and shrubs and some perennials. The process simulates natural processes in the plant's native environment.

Strigose: With sharp, straight hairs, stiff and often basally swollen, that are closely and flatly pressed against a leaf or stem.

Subcapitate: Said of a head of flowers that is not aggregated densely, somewhat loose or lax.

Suborbicular: Nearly circular, typically somewhat broadened at one point, usually near the point of attachment.

Subshrub: A perennial plant having stems that are woody at the base or a very low shrub that may be referred to as a perennial.

Subspecies: A major subdivision of a species, ranking between species and variety. It has somewhat varying connotations, depending on the user of the term, and often implies a distinct geographic distribution for the taxon.

Succulent: Having fleshy tissues that conserve moisture.

Suffrutescent: Pertaining to stems that are woody at the base and produce herbaceous shoots perennially.

Taproot: A large, main root growing straight down and giving off small side roots.

Tender annual: A plant with only one growing season; incapable of resisting cold or other adverse growing conditions.

Thicket: A dense growth of shrubs, underbrush, or small trees.

Throat: The opening into a flower with fused petals where the unfused petal tips join the tube, or fused portion.

Tomentose: Densely woolly or pubescent; with matted, soft woollike hairiness.

Tomentulose: Somewhat or delicately tomentose.

Trifoliolate: Three-leaved, as in *Trillium*.

Umbel: An inflorescence typical of the carrot family in which the axis is very much contracted so that the stalk appears to spring from the same point to form a flat or rounded flower cluster.

Variety: A subdivision of a species, officially ranking between subspecies and forma when these are also used. It is often used for a major subdivision of a species (sometimes in the sense of subspecies) and has also frequently been used in the sense of form (forma). Before the term *cultivar* was coined, *variety* could also have the sense of that term, designating a variant of horticultural origin of importance.

Verticillaster: A false whorl, applied to a pair of opposite cymes that are more or less continuous and seem to surround the stem, common in the mint family.

Vine: Any plant with a long stem that grows along the ground or climbs a wall or other support by means of stems, tendrils, or leaf petioles that twist around supports, or by aerial roots, hooked thorns, or tiny adhesive discs.

Whorl: A group of parts (as leaves or petals) encircling an axis and especially a plant stem.

Wing: A thin, dry, or membranaceous expansion or flat extension or appendage of an organ (e.g. stem or fruit); also the lateral petals of a pea flower.

Zygomorphic: Said of flowers that can be divided into two symmetrical halves only when cut from tip to base in a vertical plane (e.g. snapdragon, penstemon).

Moon carrot.

Glossary terms reprinted with permission from:

Sixty-four definitions from *Taxonomy of Vascular Plants* by George H. M. Lawrence, Appendix II, pp. 737–75. Copyright 1951 by The Macmillan Company. Reprinted by permission of Pearson Education, Inc.

Bailey/Hortus Third, Glossary of Botanical Terms, pp. 1208–25. Copyright 1976 by Macmillan Publishing Company. Reprinted with permission of John Wiley & Sons, Inc.

Botanical Latin by William T. Stearn. Copyright 1978 by David & Charles. Reprinted with permission of David & Charles.

Biology-Online.org:
www.biology-online.org

Clemson University Glossary of Intellectual Property Rights:
www.clemson.edu/research/ottSite/ottStart_IntelectDefs.htm#p

Glossary of Biotechnology and Genetic Engineering:
www.fao.org/docrep/003/X3910E/X3910E00.htm

Denver Water Department, *Xeriscape Plant Guide*. Golden, CO: Fulcrum Publishing, 1998.

Illustrators and Photographers

Botanical Illustrators

Claudia A. Anderson, 152

Priscilla Baldwin, 30, 62, 92

Janice H. Baucum, 134

Karla Beatty, 110

Stephanie Busby, 126

Karen Cleaver, 36

Beverly Coogan, 32, 118, 138

Kathy Cranmer, 136

Linda Darcy, front cover, 158

Nancy N. DeGuire, 144

Susan DiMarchi, i, 40, 148, 162

Susan T. Fisher, 104

Ann A. Fleming, 46, 74, 94

Sharon Z. Garrett, 98

Susan Halstedt, front cover, 96

Sharon Hegner, 142

Mervi Hjelmroos-Koski, 34

Kate Hurley Morton, 70

Jayme S. Irvin, 42, 86, 90

Renee L. Jorgensen, 68, 78, 156, 169

Libby Kyer, 38, 114, 122

Martha J. Long, 84

Donna Loomis, 52

Susan G. Lyons, 13, 14, 44

Debra Mallory, 18, 150

Melissa L. Martin, 102

Jill Moring, 88, 116, 124, 128, 164

Susan B. Olson, front cover flap, 8, 48, 76, 109, 112

Angela W. Overy, 57, 80

Sheila Payne, 82

Sandra J. Penfound, 24, 58, 146, 154

Annie M. Reiser, 20, 100

Susan Rubin, 50, 161, 166

Roy L. Sanford, 66

Constance Sayas, 54, 106

Margaret A. Sjoden, 22, 140, back cover flap

Joan Sommerfeld, 26, 130

Julie Anne Sprinkle, 28, 60, 72, 210

Heidi Taylor, 16, 132

Julie Anne Terry, 64

Janet C. Warren, 120

Photographers

Ann Clark, 43 (right)

Ray Daugherty, i (upper left), 74, 85 (right), 89 (right), 124, 145

Pat Hayward, vi, 135, 137, 151, back cover

Robert Heapes, 165

Shalene Hiller Navant, 10 (middle)

Mervi Hjelmroos-Koski, 48

Dan Johnson, i (middle), iv, 26, 29, 44, 56, 62, 63, 69 (right), 116, 120, 140, 141 (right), 158, 159

Panayoti Kelaidis, 36, 91 (right), 97 (left), 114, 125 (left), 141 (left), 149 (right)

James E. Klett, 8 (top), 17 (left), 21 (left), 37 (left), 90, 117, 130

Charles Mann, 64, 73, 86, 96

Harriett McMillan, 58, 133

Diana Reavis, i (right), 20, 22, 23 (right), 34, 45 (right), 60, 61, 113 (right), 123 (left), 152, 157 (left)

Al Rollinger, 33 (right), 46, 47 (left and right), 168

Judy Sedbrook, i (lower left), 13 (left), 17 (right), 23 (left), 27 (left), 28, 29 (bottom), 31 (middle), 53 (middle left), 57 (right), 71 (left), 72, 75 (right), 79 (right), 97 (right), 99, 106, 107 (right), 110, 131 (right), 143 (left and right), 161 (bottom), 167 (right), 169 (bottom left), 191

David Staats, 13 (bottom), 14, 25 (left and right), 31 (right), 43 (left), 54, 55 (middle and right), 75 (left), 66, 128, 156

Randy Tatroe, 57 (center top), 59, 91 (left), 93 (right), 103 (left), 107 (left), 160, 166, 167 (left)

David Winger, iii, 4, 7, 8 (bottom), 9 (all), 10 (top and bottom), 12, 13 (upper middle and right), 15 (left and right), 16, 18, 19 (left and right), 21 (right), 24, 27, 30, 31 (left), 33 (left), 35, 37 (right), 38, 39 (right), 40, 41, 42, 45 (left), 49, 50, 51 (left and right), 52, 53 (left, middle right, right), 55 (left), 57 (left, center bottom), 65 (left and right), 67 (left and right), 68, 69 (left), 70, 71 (right), 76, 77 (left and right), 78, 79 (left), 80, 81 (left and right), 82, 83, 84, 85 (left), 87 (left and right), 88, 89 (left), 92, 93 (left), 94, 95, 98, 100, 101 (left and right), 102, 103 (right), 104, 105, 108, 109 (top and bottom), 111, 112, 113 (left), 115 (left and right), 118, 119, 121 (left and right), 122, 123 (right), 125 (right), 126, 127 (left and right), 129 (left and right), 131 (left), 132, 134, 136, 138, 139, 142, 144, 146, 147 (left and right), 148, 149 (left), 150, 153, 154, 155, 157 (right), 161 (top), 162, 163, 164, 169 (top left, top right, and bottom right), 200

Susan Yetter, 32, 39 (left)

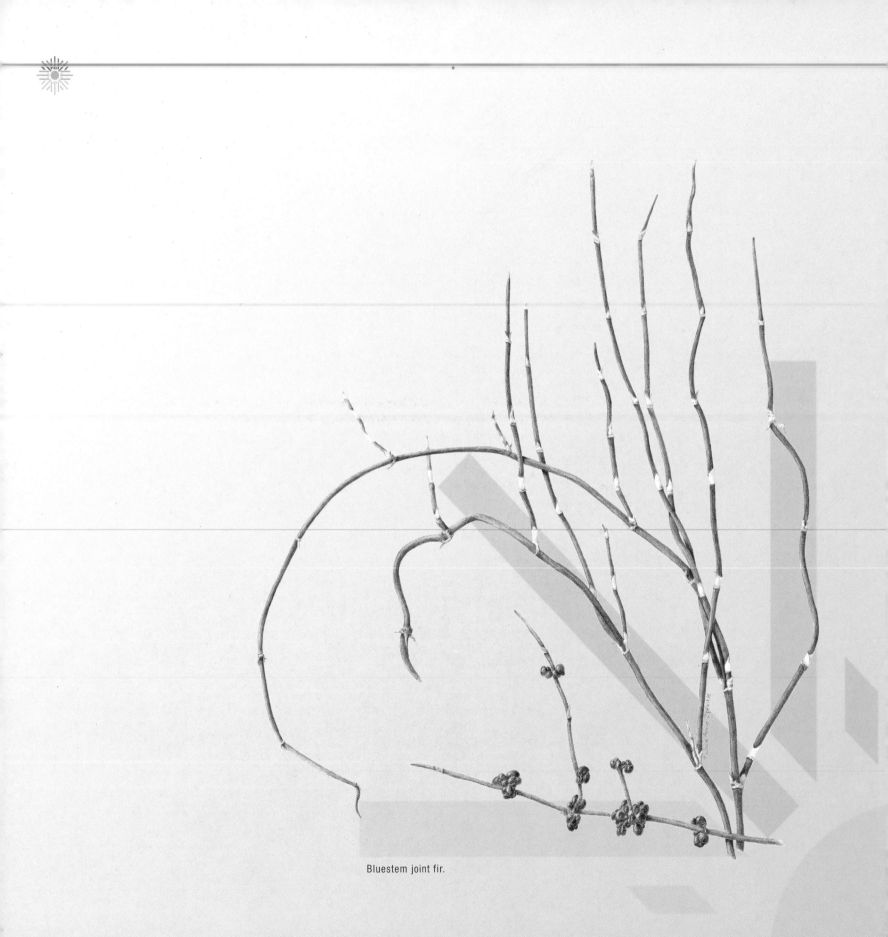

Bluestem joint fir.